The Mystery Fancier
May-June 1983

$2.50

vol.7
no.3

The Mystery Fancier

Volume 7, Number 3
May/June 1983

TABLE OF CONTENTS

MYSTERIOUSLY SPEAKING	Page 1
Closing the Gap: A Critique By John Nieminski	Page 6
The Fattest Man in the Medical Profession By Bob Sampson	Page 16
Deadly Edges of the Gay Blade By Martha Alderson	Page 23
REEL MURDERS Movie Reviews by Walter Albert	Page 29
VERDICTS Book Reviews	Page 32
THE DOCUMENTS IN THE CASE Letters	Page 43

The Mystery Fancier
(USPS:428-590)
is edited and published bi-monthly by
Guy M. Townsend
1711 Clifty Drive
Madison, IN 47250

SUBSCRIPTION RATES: Second-class mail, U.S. and Canada, $12.00 per year (6 issues); first-class mail, U.S. and Canada, $15.00; overseas surface mail, $12.00; overseas air mail, $18.00. Overseas subscribers please pay in international money order, check drawn on U.S. bank, or currency; no checks drawn on foreign banks, please.

Single copy price: $2.50

Second-class postage paid at Madison, Indiana

Copyright 1982 by Guy M. Townsend
All rights reserved for contributors
ISSN:0146-3160

Mysteriously Speaking...

The Droodians among us seem to have calmed down a bit, so I think I'll stir them up with a brief mention of a clipping sent to me by Frank Canfield, Jr. The clip, from the **Des Moines Sunday Register** of 24 April 1983, is entitled "Did notorious Harvard murder hold clue to Dickens' unfinished 'Mystery of Edwin Drood'?" and is identified as being a reprint of an article written by Canadian free-lance writer Jim Garner for **Harvard Magazine**. While back issues of the **Sunday Register** may be difficult to come by in any neck of the woods beyond the immediate vicinity of Des Moines, **Harvard Magazine** should be available in just about any pretentious library in the country. Those of you who prefer to give pretentious institutions the same wide berth that you give pretentious individuals will have to content yourselves with this précis. Here goes:

In early 1868, while on a visit to the United States, Charles Dickens was shown the site, in Harvard Medical School, where one John White Webster, a professor of chemistry and mineralogy, had, some eighteen years earlier, smashed in the head and dismembered the body of Dr. George Parkman following a quarrel about a long-standing financial debt owed by the former to the latter. Dickens' own magazine, **All the Year Round**, had run "a detailed article" on the murder (by Sir James Emerson Tennent) only the year before, so Dickens was familiar with the particulars of the case even before his visit. Indeed, he had met the murderer, Webster, during a visit to the U.S. in 1842, and, Garner opines, "he may well have met the murdered man, too."

It was two years after Dickens' return to England that he began to write his **Mystery of Edwin Drood**, and, of course, he died when the work was only half completed, leaving behind the most exquisite mystery our genre has known or probably ever will know. [It is my personal opinion that an uncompleted **Drood** is a far, far better thing for us to have than a completed **Drood** ever could have been. No matter how wonderful a mystery story **Drood** might have been had Dickens lived to complete it, it could not possibly have produced as much pleasure as the uncompleted **Drood** has done.] Garner contends, as the title of the newspaper article indicates, that the solution to the disappearance of young Edwin Drood in "Cloisterham" is to be found on this side of the Atlantic--in Cambridge, Massachusetts, to be precise--and he points out a number of striking parallels between the Webster case and the Drood case, all of which lead him to conclude that Drood was indeed murdered and that his murderer was the Webster character in his novel--John Jasper.

Garner admits that "it is, of course, easy to wring out of the two tales every possible coincidence and point to them as evidence that the Parkman case was Dickens' source, while ignoring disparities as reflective of the novelist's artistic license. Yet all authors, even those of genius, must get their inspiration somewhere."

There is another mystery here, Garner asserts, and that is how this solution to The Great Drood Question could have escaped the notice of dedicated Droodians for more than a century. Naturally, Garner has his own answer ready: "We must remember that the great New England literary elite had been deeply shocked by Webster's crime. They wanted Parkman and Webster to stay buried, even if that meant burying the source of 'The Mystery of Edwin Drood.'

"One can readily understand a situation in which the Americans, who knew very well how Dickens got his inspiration, would keep the knowledge to themselves, while the English, anxious to learn every facet of the background of Drood, could overlook the scanty clues available to them."

When I first began publishing **TMF** back in 1976 (the Preview Issue was dated November of that year and actually came out on time), I had no expectation that it would ever have a very large readership. When, at the end of a year's publication, the magazine had comfortably topped the magical number 100, I was pleased with its progress, and during the next several years its circulation never climbed very high above 200. Then, a couple of years back, I got the urge to beef up the circulation. For this I had three motives. First, I have a high, if immodest, opinion of **TMF**, and I would like to see such a splendid publication read more widely by mystery fans. Second, I have long wanted to be able to pay contributors for the work they do for **TMF**, even if that payment has to be little more than a token amount. And third, I would eventually like to realize some financial return from the considerable amount of time and money that I have poured into this publication over the years.

For all these reasons, I decided to blitz the mystery world and rake in hundreds of new subscribers. Five hundred, I thought, was a modest expectation, and I had secret hopes that **TMF** might even top one thousand. I did everything I could think of. I sent flyers to about five thousand individuals and libraries, at a cost of about thirty cents a head. I sent out about a thousand free issues of the magazine to prospective subscribers (in two separate mailings of about five hundred each), at a cost which I refuse to calculate even now. I placed ads in other mystery publications, and some mystery publishers even generously allowed me to insert flyers in their own magazines. All of which cost me literally thousands of dollars--and netted me what? Fewer than one hundred permanent new subscribers. At the end of the last volume, **TMF** had jumped to more than four hundred paying subscribers, but a great number of the Johnny-Come-Latelies chose not to renew for volume seven, and the **TMF** crew now consists of just over three hundred faithful. So I am finally giving up on two of the three things that motivated me to try to increase **TMF**'s subscription roll: we won't be reaching any great number of mystery fans, and I won't be making much money off the magazine. But I hate to give up on the third motivation--paying contributors--and that brings me to the point of this rambling disquisition.

I would still like to begin paying contributors for their articles and reviews, but I simply can't afford to do so out of the income from three hundred subscriptions at current rates. For its first two years, annual subscriptions to **TMF** were $7.50. I jumped the price to $9.00

for volume three and held it there for volume four as well, before going to $12.00 with volume five. There it has sat for the past three years. I resisted the temptation to raise it again with volume seven (thereby keeping with the every-other-volume increase schedule I had followed until then), largely because that remarkable financial wizard, Ronald Reagan, has, by the brilliant stroke of throwing millions of Americans out of work, managed to bring inflation under control, and I didn't rightly see how I could ask you folks to pay me more money for a product that I wasn't having to pay more money to produce. [I don't count the cost of purchasing printing presses, graphics cameras, computers, printers, and the like, since I took those steps on my own without consultation with or urging from the rest of you folks.] But if I can't make more money by acquiring more subscribers--and I can't--then the only way I can raise the money to pay contributors is by raising the subscription rate. But, since it appears that Reagan is determined to keep down inflation by any sacrifice necessary (so long as said sacrifice is made by someone other than himself or his well-to-do friends), I am extremely reluctant to undertake an increase in the subscription rate effective with volume eight until I have sounded out the readership on the question.

Frankly, **TMF**'s current readership represents a hard core of mystery fans, most of whom would probably go along with a rate increase, albeit perhaps not without some grumbling, so I could probably get away with jacking up the price without so much as a howdy-do. But, by golly, we're in this thing together--**TMF** is kept alive as much by your support as by my efforts--and I don't want to take such a step without first consulting you people.

I would like to raise the cost of subscriptions by $3.00 across the board, effective with **TMF** 8:1. That is, regular second-class subscriptions (and overseas surface-mail subscriptions) would go from $12.00 to $15.00; first-class domestic (and Canadian) subscriptions would go from $15.00 to $18.00; and air-mail overseas subscriptions would go from $18.00 to $21.00. This would bring in perhaps another thousand dollars each year.

At six issues per year, this will give me an extra $166.67 per issue from which to pay contributors. What I have in mind is paying half a cent per word for articles, columns, and reviews. My very strong inclination was to propose half a cent for articles and a quarter of a cent for reviews, since I firmly believe that it is more difficult to write an article than it is to write reviews of comparable length, but I know this would raise some hackles, so what I am proposing is a flat, across-the-board payment of half a cent per.

Except for letters. No pay for letters, folks. I'm sure everyone will agree with this, although each of us would probably express his reasons differently.

Each issue of **TMF** contains about 30,000 words. **TMF** 7:2 was typical, and its total was 29,213, give or take a few syllables. Of these, 6,123 were in the letters section and 1,047 were in "Mysteriously Speaking ...," so only 22,043 words would actually have been eligible for payment, had the proposed payment policy been in effect when the issue was published. At half a cent per word, the total of payments for that issue would have come to $110.22, leaving a surplus of $56.45--which surplus I would have salted away in the burgeoning numbered Swiss bank account in which I deposit all my profits from this enterprise.

So there you have it, folks. You must tell me whether you want to keep the subscription rates where they are and let the people whose hard work edifies and entertains you every other month go on working for nothing, or whether you are willing to see the rates raised a notch with the understanding that the increase is to be used principally to give a little financial reward to those deserving fellows (and fellettes). This rate increase is not for me--or even for my creditors. It is for the people who really make **TMF** possible.

Please take the time to drop me a note expressing your sentiments on the subject--a simple "Yes" or "No" scrawled on a postcard will be sufficient to let me know whether you are for or against the increase. If you wish, you may even deduct the cost of the card or letter from your next year's renewal check. These editorial appeals for responses have a notoriously low rate of return, so I don't expect to hear from all of you, or even a majority, but I am going to be guided by the responses that I do get, provided there is a pronounced leaning in either direction, and if some of you definitely would not renew if the subscription rates were increased by $3.00, be sure to let me know.

I would also like to hear from **TMF**'s regular contributors as to how they feel about the proposed increase.

Before ending this already too long editorial column, I've a number of things on hand that I need to mention, some of which have been gathering dust on my desk for an embarrassingly long time. Here, in no particular order, goes:

I loved it when John D. MacDonald's Travis McGee books appeared first in paperback and only later between hard covers. But, as you all know, this changed several years back and now if you want to read the latest McGee as soon as possible you have to buy (or borrow) the more expensive hardbound edition. Those of us long on patience can wait for the paperback, which brings me to my point--the soft cover edition of **Cinnamon Skin** will go on sale 1 July for $3.50 (from Fawcett, of course).

A few weeks back I received in the mail a postcard announcing the opening of a new mystery bookstore. It's name is either "Murder Under Cover, Inc." or "Kate's Mystery Books" (the card is somewhat ambiguous on this point), and it is located at 2211 Massachusetts Ave., Cambridge, MA 02140 (phone:617/491-2660). I'll give you the two other pieces of information which appear on the card, and then you'll know as much as I do: "GRAND OPENING 5-8 Friday the 13th of MAY, KATE MATTES, proprietress," and "Summer Hours: 12-7 Wednesday-Saturday, 1-6 Sunday."

Bjarne Nielsen, who produces the Danish magazine **Pinkerton**, has recently published a translation of **My Dear Watson**, Henry Lauritzen's appreciation of Sherlock Holmes's sadly underrated companion. The short (33 page) book is a must for Sherlockians. It is handsomely produced on high-quality glossy paper, and is replete with illustrations. The book has paper covers, but this doesn't mean what you probably think it does. This is a quality product, well worth the $13.00 US Nielsen is selling it for. The English edition is limited to 413 copies, same as the 1954 Danish original. Nielsen did the translation himself. His address is Nansensgade 68, 1366 Kobenhavn K, DENMARK.

I expect that the pulp fans among you are already acquainted with this next item, but here it is, anyway. Bernard A. Drew (53 Gilmore Ave., Great Barrington, MA 01230) has been gathering together stories from the pulps by various pulp writers and publishing them in facsimile, together with introductions by Drew himself. Fittingly, these publications, which appear under the general title of **Attic Revivals,** are printed on newsprint, the nearest you can get to pulp today, and are in a saddle-stapled, 8-1/2 x 11" format. Number One features Judson

Philips, runs to 16 pages, and costs $1.50 (add fifty cents per issue for postage). Number Two features Lester Dent and Herman Petersen, is 32 pages long, and costs $3.50. Number Three features Joseph W. Musgrave's Sheena, Queen of the Jungle, is 16 pages in length, and costs $2.50. Number Four/Five is a double issue featuring Walter Gibson and others, is 16 pages long, and costs $2.50. Number Six, featuring Anthony M. Rud, is also 16 pages long; I don't have a price on it, but I would guess $2.50.

And I can't mention pulps without giving another plug to Tom Johnson's fine publication, **Echoes**, the seventh issue of which has just arrived. This is a must for pulp fans. Single issues are $2.25, and a three-issue subscription is $6.50. If Tom can get enough subscribers, he plans to lower the subscription rate, so there's some extra incentive for signing up now.

Walker, St. Martin's, and Doubleday are presently the only hardcover publishers who are devoting a great deal of effort to publishing a substantial line of mysteries. Walker has lately come across with several books of particular interest to me. One is Jon Breen's splendid first novel, **Listen for the Click**, which Mike Nevins reviews in this issue. Another is Max Collins' second Mallory novel, **No Cure for Death**, which I liked even better than the first one. Both Jon and Max are Mystery Fanciers, so it is a double pleasure to see them doing so well. Both books are $12.95. Will Harriss is not one of us, but, after reading his first novel, **The Bay Psalm Book Murder**, I wish he was. For a first effort, this is truly superb; I can hardly wait for the next one. Also from Walker and also $12.95.

And one final item. Paul Bishop publishes an apazine called **The Thieftaker Journals** for DAPA-EM, the mystery amateur publication association (from which I recently departed, under a cloud, of course). Paul generally does very good work, but with his last issue he has really outdone himself. Volume two, number four (May 1983) is a separate magazine in its own right, and a beautiful one at that. It is 8-1/2 x 11", saddle stapled, printed on slick paper and profusely illustrated throughout, and bound in a bright green cover stock. Entitled "The Sport of Sleuths," it is devoted to mysteries and racing, and if I didn't already have a copy (through Paul's generosity) I'd be begging him to sell me one. Its sixteen pages plus cover are easily worth several bucks. Write Paul and see if he has any extra copies for sale.

And that, believe it or not, is all I've got to say for this issue. Next time I'll try to hold myself to a more modest page or two.

Closing the Gap: A Critique

John Nieminski

Michael L. Cook, comp. **Monthly Murders.** Greenwood Press, 1982, 1147 + xvii pp., $49.50.

In the field of science fiction, the indexing of genre periodicals is perhaps the most prominent manifestation of that form of scholarly endeavor known as "sercon fanac." Checklists of one kind or another dotted the pages of the early fanzines of the 1930s, and by the late 1940s, when the number of sf magazines being published grew, more elaborate compilations began to appear. Some thirty-eight such works, issued over a twenty-five year span, are described in **SF Bibliographies** by Robert E. Briney and Edward Wood (Chicago: Advent, 1972), ranging in type from highly specialized listings like T.G.L. Cockcroft's **Index to the Verse in Weird Tales** (1960) to the late Donald B. Day's monumental 1952 **Index to the Science Fiction Magazines, 1926-1950,** which covered in exhaustive detail the contents of approximately fifty specialty periodicals. Others have made their way into print since then, and the total number published must by now be close to half a hundred.

By comparison, indexing in the mystery fiction field is a late emerging phenomenon. Jon L. Breen's **What About Murder?** (Metuchen, N.J.: The Scarecrow Press, 1981) cites in its "Reference Books" section only three comparable efforts, all of recent vintage: the late William J. Clark's 1971 **Author Index to Doc Savage Magazine,** and this reviewer's **EQMM 350** (1973) and **The Saint Magazine Index** (1980). And to this grouping can now be added E.R. Hagemann's **Comprehensive Index to Black Mask, 1920-1951,** published last year by Bowling Green State University Popular Press. Not listed by Breen, probably because of the extremely limited distribution it was given, is a detailed **Index of Dime Detective Magazine** compiled by Elmore H. Mundell a few years ago, and mention can also be made of items of lesser scope which have appeared from time to time in the pages of fan magazines. Representative examples of the latter include Robert E. Briney's **Mystery Book Magazine** index in **The Armchair Detective** (August 1975) and the late Don Miller's "Ellery Queen's Mystery Magazine--1975 Index" in the 15 December 1975 issue of **The Mystery Nook.** But even a complete listing of these fugitive efforts would be a short one compared to the substantial body of periodical reference works produced thus far by science fiction aficionados, and in coverage one in no way as comprehensive.

Monthly Murders, which appeared last spring, is the first major attempt to index the contents of any sizeable number of the many

English-language mystery genre magazines published over the years. Given the work involved in compiling a listing of its proportions and the cost of producing a volume of its size, it is likely to stand for some time as the only guide of its type. For this reason a detailed examination of its offerings may be of interest both to prospective purchasers and to library-copy users, as well as those awaiting the appearance of a promised companion volume which will reportedly cover the bulk of those periodicals not indexed here, including the pulps.

Physically, the book is a hefty tome, approximately 2-1/2" thick and measuring 6-1/2" X 9-1/2" in width and height. As with most reference works published these days, it comes without dustjacket, but it is sturdily encased in an attractive bright red binding. The volume lays flat when opened to any but the first and last few pages and is otherwise easy to wield despite its bulk. This reviewer's copy has held up well under repeated usage (including the extensive accuracy-sampling exercise described below), with no signs of wear or loosening in the spine area. Readers accustomed to more fragile examples of the bookbinder's art (e.g., St. Martin's **Twentieth Century Crime and Mystery Writers**) will be pleased with the production job done by Greenwood Press.

Except for the preliminary pages, the title headings in the chronological listing section, and the running heads throughout, all of which feature composed typefaces, the text is typewritten copy reproduced by photo-offset printing. The typing is neatly done and readable without strain, and the material carried in the two major sections is laid out with a welcome abundance of white space and with no crowding in evidence. The smooth, glare-free paper used has a tendency to retain wrinkles produced by moist fingertips, sometimes permanently, but it accepts pencilled notations readily, without smearing or tearing.

The subtitle appearing on the cover and on the title page—"A Checklist and Chronological Listing of Fiction in the Digest-Size Mystery Magazines in the United States and England"—is something of a misnomer. As indicated with examples below, some larger than digest-size magazines are covered, several are in whole or part outside the mystery genre, and some non-fiction material is indexed. And more accurately, the book is a listing of magazine tables of contents, cross-referenced by code symbols to an author section where that data is reconstituted alpahbetically by title. The subtitle is by no means misleading, however, and in any case the compiler makes quite clear the actual scope of the work in his introduction and "User's Guide" and in his headnotes to each magazine entry.

And that scope is impressive indeed, extending as it does to the principal contents of some 110 magazines published here and in England under a total of 130 different titles. Of the 110, 92 are American and 18 British, several of the latter constituting overseas editions of American publications like **EQMM**, **AHMM** and others. Of that same number, 86 are indexed in their entirety, or presumably so; only occasionally is it specifically stated that the coverage of a given run is complete. Incomplete runs are clearly identified, however (most frequently with the statement "No data available" for a given number), as are the two or three issues for which the contents listings are partial only. And whenever some doubt exists, the compiler so indicates. All told, table-of-contents data is provided for 2651 issues in whole or part. Extrapolating from the information furnished, it appears that the 2651 represent approximately 95% of all the issues published under the 130 titles, a very respectable figure given the now almost complete unavailability of some of the older and more obscure magazines.

The "Chronological Listing of Contents," the first of the volume's two major sections, provides the following data for each of the 110 serials covered: the magazine title; a two-letter alpha code used for cross-referencing to the author section; and a brief headnote which lists publisher names and addresses and carries, as appropriate, information concerning title changes, dating anomalies, etc. For each individual issue indexed, the user is provided with the issue date, the volume and/or number, the cover price, and the title and author of each item indexed. The ordering of the latter generally follows that of the magazine contents pages themselves, with some few exceptions where they are listed alphabetically by author, and some non-fiction entries are annotated to reflect their content (e.g., true crime, verse, puzzle, etc.). Of all the informatiopn furnished in this section, the cover price seems to be the least necessary, and the most obvious omission is the absence of a citation of the number of pages carried in a given issue, which would be helpful in determining if copies owned are full and complete.

Among the issues indexed in the "Chronological Listing" are a small number which appeared in formats other than digest-size, including the bedsheet variety featured for a time by **Manhunt** and **Alfred Hitchcock's Mystery Magazine**, and a handful of others in the intermediate size range. Their exclusion on this basis would clearly serve no useful purpose. Less justifiable, perhaps, is the indexing of the four early-1930s issues of **Mystery League**, covered here despite their oversize dimensions for the reason that "many erroneously consider [it] to be the predecessor to **Ellery Queen's Mystery Magazine**." This seems hardly sufficient, but their presence does no harm, even though the uninformed user will conclude that the magazine carried only fiction. For a complete citation of **Mystery League**'s still interesting non-fiction features, one has to turn elsewhere, such as to the listing which appears in Francis M. Nevins's **Royal Bloodline** (Bowling Green, OH: Bowling Green University Popular Press, 1974).

Of all the mystery fiction periodicals indexed in the "Chronological Listing," a small number are borderline specimens, some more so than others. The first five issues of **Saturn Web**, for example, carried nothing but science fiction. A few, like **Shock**, featured mixed contents, while others, such as **Weird Mystery, Startling Mystery**, and **The Haunt of Horror**, leaned heavily in the direction of tales of the macabre. These and several more like them are here indexed in full, including one or two that could as easily have been omitted because of the preponderance in their pages of fantasy or supernatural stories. None is totally beyond the pale, however, and in any case headnotes alert the user to their presence and content. Purists who might be inclined to question the decision to include them are reminded that even a magazine as solidly in the mystery genre as **EQMM** occasionally offers up as a change of pace similarly borderline material.

About a third of the volume is given over to the second major section, the "Index by Author." Here, listed in alphabetical order, are the by-lined names of the authors of the contents-page entries carried in the "Chronological Listing." Each author's entries are likewise alpahbetized and coded to reflect the magazines and the issues in which they appear. (About this feature, more below.) Approximately 120 pseudonymns are identified and are cross-referenced to their users' real names. This data is by no means exhaustive (nor is it claimed to be), and some errors have crept in and a few citations are misleading. Among the omissions which may be mentioned are the following, many of which are taken from **Twentieth Century Crime and Mystery Writers,** the same source used by the compiler for most of those that he does cite:

> Steve April = Leonard S. Zinsberg
> Evelyn Bond = Morris Hershman
> Ernest Bramah = Ernest Bramah Smith
> Michael Brett = Miles Tripp
> Leo Bruce = Rupert Croft-Cooke
> Duffy Carpenter = John J. Hurley
> James Hadley Chase = René Raymond
> John Crowe = Dennis Lynds
> Mark Dane = Michael Avallone
> Peter Friday = Herbert Harris
> "Pat Hand" = Thomas B. Costain
> Martin Ivory = James M. Ullman
> Milward Kennedy = Milward Burge
> Thomas Kyd = Alfred B. Harbage
> Michael Moore = Herbert Harris
> Guy Nedmon = Ned Guymon
> Rhona Petrie = Eileen Buchanan
> S.S. Rafferty = John J. Hurley
> Jack Ritchie = John G. Reitci
> Mark Sadler = Dennis Lynds
> Joseph Shearing = Gabrielle Margaret Vere Campbell
> Robert Traver = John J. Voelker
> Simon Troy = Thurman Warriner

Further, since their marriages, Brèni James writes as Brèni Pevehouse and Eugenia Klein as Eugenia Klein Gingold (when they write at all), but their maiden and married names are not cross-referenced; "Clifford Ashdown" is identified as R. Austin Freeman alone, even though the pseudonym masked a collaboration with John J. Pitcairn; it is not probable that J.I.M. Stewart, more commonly known as Michael Innes, was in fact the J.M. Stewart who authored four stories in **John Creasey Mystery Magazine** and one in **London Mystery Magazine,** all in the late 1950s (a reading of the latter tale should quickly disabuse anyone of that notion); it seems hardly likely, as claimed here, that Lester del Rey ever wrote as Paul W. Fairman; and, despite the flat out attribution on page 921, Leslie Charteris is most assuredly not Harry Harrison--not even the Harry Harrison credited in the "Index by Author" with five stories in **The Saint Mystery Magazine.** (If anything, the opposite is more probably the case, at least on occasion; Harrison, the science fiction writer, is widely rumored to have ghosted Charteris's 1964 Simon Templar novel, **Vendetta for the Saint.)**

And last, three of the Doc Savage stories attributed to Lester Dent were in fact authored by William Bogart, or so say several other printed sources, including Philip José Farmer's **Doc Savage: His Apocalyptic Life** (New York: Doubleday, 1975); fifteen of the Shadow novels here credited to Walter Gibson appear to have been written by Bruce Elliott instead, according to information carried in Gibson's **Shadow Scrapbook** (New York: Harcourt Brace Jovanovich, 1979); and Walter and Jean Shine's **Bibliography of the Published Works of John D. MacDonald** (Gainesville, FL: Patrons of the Libraries, University of Florida, 1980) cites some fourteen stories by that author which appeared under various pseudonyms in **Doc Savage Magazine** and **The Shadow,** all of which are indexed here but are not so identified. Data on other "house names" is similarly meager.

All told, the "Index by Author" carries some 27,000 listings. The number of discretely different items indexed is somewhat smaller, however, since that figure includes reprints, with or without title changes. The latter are here identified by the word "same," an occasionally misleading designation since it is similarly used for multiple entries of different items with common titles (e.g., Michael Avallone's "Ed Noon's Minute Mysteries" and Talbot C. Hatch's "Guess Who?" quizzes). Items reprinted under different titles are not so identified, and separate entries appear for each without cross-referencing, whether the changes are nominal or substantial. Thus, the listing for Ellery Queen cites both "The Case Against Carroll" and "The Case Against Carell"; that for Freeman Wills Crofts both "The Hunt Ball" and "The Hunt Ball Murder"; and that for Roy Vickers both "The Case of the Twelve Minute Grave" and "The Twelve Minute Grave." There are many such examples. Less discernable title changes also abound, particularly in the listings for those writers with substantial numbers of entries appearing in more than one or two magazines (nine such are carried in the Agatha Christie citations alone), and their unidentified presence will occasionally serve to disappoint those who use the index to track down unread stories by favorite authors.

As indicated above, magazine issue dates are not cited in the entries in the "Index by Author," and to learn in which issue a given item appeared, it is necessary to refer back to the "Chronological Listing." To accomplish this, one uses the two-letter alpha code mentioned earlier. By way of example, the citation "MS 26 4" for the Grover Brinkman story, "The Tin Coffin," directs the user to **Mike Shane Mystery Magazine** in the "Chronological Listing," and therein to the table-of-contents display for Vol. 26, No. 4, where it will be discovered that "The Tin Coffin" appeared in **MSMM**'s March 1970 issue. Stated thus, the finding process sounds simple enough, if slightly awkward, and occasionally it is. More frequently, however, locating a given issue can be a frustrating and time consuming exercise, for reasons having to do with the manner in which the codes are assigned and the keys displayed.

To illustrate further, one actually begins by determining which of the 110 magazines is coded "MS," using one of two keys provided. Pages 761-763, located conveniently near the "Index by Author," carry an "Alphabetical Listing of Magazines, including Changed Titles and Code Designations" to which one can initially refer. Here (where four of the magazine titles are slightly out of alphabetical sequence), scanning the unalphabetized codes will reveal eventually that "MS" is indeed **Mike Shayne Mystery Magazine**, as one might assume from the abbreviation. But, since the key does not specify which page to turn to to find the magazine in the "Chronological Listing," this is actually of little help. For the latter, one must turn instead to the "Contents" section in the front of the book. There, the codes **are** listed in alphabetical order, but further scanning is required since they are listed in parentheses **after** each title. Finding that "MS" is **Shayne** and that the magazine's table-of-contents listings begin on page 493, one turns thereto and from that starting point flips on ahead, glancing all the while at the center area of each succeeding page where volumes and numbers are cited, until Vol. 26, No. 4 is spotted, in this instance on page 525. At which point the search, at long last, ends.

Since the magazine titles are carried in the running heads in the "Chronological Listings," users who gain familiarity with the coding designations can in some instances speed up the search process by going directly to that section, particularly when looking for magazines with listings as lengthy as those for **EQMM, AHMM,** and **MSMM,** which are easily spotted. But because the ordering of the magazines in that section is not alphabetical by title but by assigned code (for example, **Shell Scott Mystery Magazine,** coded SO, appears between **Startling Mystery,** coded SN, and **Suspect Detective Stories,** coded SP), more often than not they will be forced to turn back to the "Contents" section for guidance. It is not all that clear why the codes listed in that section do not precede the titles; nor why they are not also carried in the running heads in the "Chronological Listing," a feature which would be most helpful.

If ease of access to data is a major determinant of the usefulness of an index, the frequent user of this one will likely conclude early on that it suffers somewhat when compared to those organized along more traditional lines. Certainly there can be no question that a structuring of data which requires for its retrieval three or more steps is less efficient than one which centralizes key information. And if there are any compensating advantages to the structuring the compiler has elected to employ, they are not readily apparent. An index geared to table-of-contents listings has its attractions and can keep relatively short a related author index, but it requires, after all, no more space to cite "MS 3/70" than it does to cite "MS 26 4." In the case of **Monthly Murders,** any slight increase in the length of the author index which might result from relocating issue-date information thereto would be more than offset by the gain in space realized from the elimination of the contents-page listings, and, given the size of that section, in the same total number of pages probably afford room as well for an always useful overall title index.

The same frequent user of this work will similarly wonder early on just how accurate and reliable are its contents, since some few typos will likely be spotted here and there as one flips back and forth seeking out those elusive issue date citations. In preparation for this review, selected portions of the index were subjected to a careful screening to provide a basis for assessing just those elements. The screening took two forms: an examination of the "Index by Author" to check the alphabetizing of the entries therein, both author names and story titles; and an item-by-item comparison with the magazines themselves of a number of the entries in the "Chronological Listing" and in their subsequent carryover to the "Index by Author." In each instance, care was taken to ensure that the samples were fully representative of the totals and statistically supportive of any conclusions drawn therefrom.

In the "Index by Author" (hereinafter cited as IA), the alphabetizing of all author names and all story titles for the letters A through J was checked, that portion constituting a 50% sample of the section as a whole. In all, 95 entries were found to be out of alphabetical sequence, 25 in the case of the authors and 70 in the titles. Examples of the former include: ARNET, ROBERT between ARNOLD, H.F. and ARNOLD, A.M.; BANDY, FRANKLIN between BANISTER, MANLY and BANKIER, WILLIAM; CHECCHIA, THOMAS after CHEESMAN, HAZEL; two listings for DAVIS, NORBERT, separated by one for DAVIS, STANLEY, who belongs on the next page; and GILFORD, C.B. between GILES, KRIS and GILES, BARRY. The misalphabetized title entries include: BAKER, DOUGLAS, "Laughing on the Outside" between "Ace of Diamonds" and "Grave Mistake"; CARROLL, ROY, "The Equalizer" before "Do-Gooder"; DAVIS, RAY T., "Women's Wiles" before "Bounty," "The Lady is a Cop," and "Off Trail"; FREUND, PHILIP, "To Catch a Spy" before "The Devious Ways"; and HOWARD, ROBERT E., "King of the Night" before "The Haunter of the

Ring." In each instance, some of the incorrect sequencing is less readily apparent than in these selected examples.

The check of the IA revealed some 19 other kinds of errors as well, including the misspelling of author names (BOTTOMS, for BOTTOME, PHYLLIS; BENTLY, for BENTLEY, FREDERICK); no cross-referencing to the "Chronological Listing" (BREEN, JON L., "Adventure of the Disoriented Detective"); one misattribution (TWAIN, MARK, "The Stolen White Elephant," credited to HENRY, O.); and assorted typos (CHAFFEE, RICK, "High ane Dry"; CHRISTIE, AGATHA, "The Kidnappinf of Johnny Waverly"). These 19 together with the 95 misalphabetized entries noted above suggest that the IA carries about 230 inaccuracies, if the 50% sample is valid. As indicated below, however, the total is actually much larger.

For the accuracy assessment of the "Chronological Listing" (cited as CL from this point on), a check was made against the complete contents of 265 magazine issues, a 10% sample of the total number indexed. All told, some 2700 entries therein were compared with the citations in the CL and the IA, likewise 10% of the overall total. Included in the 265 were 28 different titles, a 25% sample, in numbers ranging from one or two for those with short runs, to as many as 80 in the case of **EQMM**. In all, 106 errors were found, grouped by type as follows:

 1 magazine titling error
 2 author misattributions
10 cross-referencing errors
10 story title omissions
21 title typos
27 author name misspellings
35 entry titling errors

Some of the 106 appear only once, in either the CL or the IA; others, especially those in the latter three categories, were found in both sections, having been carried over from the one to the other, but are here counted as one only; and none is a duplicate of any of the 19 in the IA mentioned above.

The most serious, perhaps, are the story title omissions, a complete listing of which is here provided for those who may wish to annotate their copies accordingly:

Indexed in IA but not CL: BELL, JOSEPHINE, "Experiment—", **The Saint Mystery Magazine** 10/65. Indexed in CL but not in IA: HALLIDAY, BRETT, "Murder Go Round," **MSMM** 3/79 (a story different from the one indexed as "Murder-Go-Round"); BRADFORD, MARY, "The Office Party," **AHMM** 7/76; HARRISON, HARRY, "I Always Do What Teddy Says," **EQMM** 6/65; PHAON, JERROLD, "The Outsider," **EQMM** 9/76. Indexed neither in CL nor IA: OLDE, NICHOLAS, "The Collector of Curiosities", **EQMM** 7/42; CHRISTIE, AGATHA, "Philomel Cottage," **EQMM** 4/51; WILDE, PERCIVAL, "P. Moran, Personal Observer," **EQMM** 8/51; DARDES, MARTIN, "Letter Writing as a Fine Art," **EQMM** 2/57; and BANKIER, WILLIAM, "Time Bomb," **EQMM** 8/68.

Similarly provided here is a listing of all 10 cross-referencing errors from which appropriate corrections can be made. In this instance, the index's magazine codes are cited:

ANON, "Which Is the Heir?," EQ 66, should be EQ 13 66; BELLFONTAINE, GEORGE F., "The Evil Men Speak," MS 25 4, should be 26 4; BENTLEY, NICHOLAS, "Seeing Is Believing," MS 12 3, should be 12 4; DANIELS, NORMAN, "Mr. Dove Retires," SA 10 5, should be 10 6; FRENCH, DANIEL, "Counterplot," MU 3 6, should be 3 5; GILFORD, C.B., "Key Witness," SS 1 2, should be SO 1 2; GRIFFITH, JACK, "The Sherlock Holmes of Babylon," LM 4, should be 44; HARE, CYRIL, "The Unluckiest Murderer," (none cited), should be EQ 29 5; PHILLIPOTS, EDEN, "Peters, Detective," EQ 20 (125), should be 23 (125); and RADIN, EDWARD D., "Seven Dead Women," ED 51 5, should be EQ 51 5.

The one magazine titling error noted occurs on page 669, where the subtitle of **The Saint's Choice** No. 7 (1964) is given as "The Saint's Choice of Hollywood Crime," whereas it is actually subtitled "The Saint's Choice of Radio Thrillers." And the two author misattributions will be found on page 230 in the contents page listing for the August 1951 **EQMM**. There, a dropped line eliminates the Percival Wilde story mentioned above, resulting in the crediting to Wilde of the Ernest Bramah story, "The Tragedy at Brookbend Cottage," and to Bramah the Q. Patrick story, "Town Blonde, Country Blonde." And they are so miscredited in the IA listing as well.

Several kinds of errors appear in the 35 incorrectly cited titles which surfaced in the sampling, some appearing in both the CL and the IA listings for each. A few are relatively minor in nature, such as the occasional omission of the word "The" or its substitution for "A" and the singularization of plural nouns (e.g., "Wellington" for "Wellingtons"; "Candle" for "Candles"). Others, however, are more substantial, as in these examples from **MSMM**: ALLEN, ERIC, "A Clear Case of Conscience" for ". . . Innocence"; PORGES, ARTHUR, "The Toadstool Poison" for ". . . Pigeon"; AVALLONE, MICHAEL, "Every Litter Bit Helps" for ". . . Hurts"; and MALZBERG, BARRY N., "A Small Respectful Gesture" for "A Simple . . . ." And from the **Saint**: CHARTERIS, LESLIE, "The Convenient Murder" for ". . . Monster"; SLESAR, HENRY, "The Absent Minded Professor" for ". . . Murder"; and WOOLRICH, CORNELL, "Flowers from the Sea" for ". . . the Dead." Occasionally, words are dropped, as in ABBOTT, ANTHONY, "The Perfect Crime of Mr. Digberry" (no "Perfect"); ECKELS, ROBERT EDWARD, "The Last One to Know" (no "One"); or added, as in LEE, ROLAND, "Light in the Darkness"; CAVE, HUGH B., "Naked in the Darkness." And in their carryover from the magazines to the index, the capitalization of words is frequently changed, sometimes inconsistently so.

The incidence of name misspellings seems to be the greatest in the contents-page listings, where most of the 27 uncovered in the sampling were found. If they are in fact heavily concentrated there, the smaller number sprinkled throughout the IA would not seriously impair the usefulness of that section as an aurthor locator, though there are exceptions. Of the 27, some are fairly insignificant, e.g., MACMILLAN, for MacMILLAN, PAT; GORDON A., for PRESCOTT, GORDON R.; EDMUND for ALTER, ROBERT EDMOND; and EBERHARD, for EBERHART, MIGNON G. More likely to mislead some users are such as REES, for REESE, JOHN; JACK, for ELLIS, MEL; BLOCH, for BLOCHMAN, LAWRENCE; FRANTZ, for FRANZ, JAMES R.; HARRY, for DANE, HENRY; and CAIDA, for CSIDA, JOSEPH.

Those somewhere in between include HENSEN, for HANSON, DIANA; MASTERSON, for MASTERTON, GORDON; and CLEMENS, for CLEMONS, JOHN. PROCTER, MAURICE here materializes as PROCTOR, and probably not for the first time thus in print; somehow, STEEL, KURT has become STEEL, KARL as well, with separate listings appearing under each name in the IA; and Baker Street Irregulars with long memories and short fuses will probably not take too kindly to the crediting, in both the CL and the IA, of one story by DOYLE, ARTHUR CONAN to his son ADRIAN, even if it is a non-Sherlock Holmes tale.

The 21 title typos run the gamut also. Readily apparent as such are "Bair," in "Bait for a Man-Trap" (BLOCHMAN, LAWRENCE G.); "Applies," in "Apples of the Hesperides" (CHRISTIE, AGATHA); "Torse," in "Whose Torso?" (PORGES, ARTHUR); "Chite," in "Death out of Chute 3" (MATTHEWS, CLAYTON); and "None," in "The Nine-to-Five Man" (ELLIN, STANLEY). Those perhaps less obvious include "Bloomsburg," in "The Bloomsbury Wonder" (BURKE, THOMAS); "Mortgage," in "The Missing Mortgagee" (FREEMAN, R. AUSTIN); "Tweiller," in "Mrs. Twiller Takes a Trip" (LITTLE, LAEL J.); "Higin," in "How Mr. Hogan Robbed a Bank" (STEINBECK, JOHN); and "Holligans," in "Gideon: The Hooligans" (MARRIC, J.J.). The most amusing, by far, is "The Libert of the Subjecty" (DAVIDSON, AVRAM), with its wide-ranging terminal consonant, a few of which we've all left danglin in our timeg.

Not counted as errors, but somewhat misleading nonetheless, are those title citations which mask stories published in groups of two or more under a generic heading. For example, "Tales from Home" by L.E. Behney, published in **EQMM** 4/63 and so carried in both the CL and the IA, is actually three different stories, each with its own title ("The Day of the Fair," "Cross My Heart," and "The Sound of Women Weeping"), none of which is separately listed. When the generic title is suggestive of such multiplicity of content (as in "Two More 'Tales from Home'" by the same author in **EQMM** 8/66), the user will likely recognize that duplicate entries are involved and thus be guided accordingly, though not necessarily so in every instance. But the opportunities for misinterpretation are enhanced when the generic title is more ambiguous, as in the case of "Appleby's Fables," the heading given to four individually titled short-short stories by Michael Innes published simultaneously in the May 1960 issue of **The Saint Mystery Magazine**. Readers who encounter references elsewhere to any of the four and seek them out here may conclude erroneously from the absence of citations that they are not carried in any of the magazines indexed. Other examples so treated include "The Adventures of Karmesin" (**EQMM** 12/47; two stories) and "Two Tales of Bo Raymond" (**EQMM** 7/65); all by Gerald Kersh; Philip MacDonald's "Two Exploits of Harry the Hat" (**EQMM** 2/49; two stories); and "The Two Deaths of Dr. Kang" (**EQMM** 8/57), two stories by Victor Canning.

Finally, the comparison of the 265 magazines with the listings in the CL revealed that the index as a whole actually carries more non-fiction entries (articles, true crime, poetry, and puzzles) than is suggested by the subtitle or reflected in the annotations. Only partial counts were posted during the exercise, but some 20 articles were found to be indexed and not identified as such; similarly were 5 poems encountered without annotation; and, in the case of true crime accounts, over 60 of which are so designated in the CL, 10 more surfaced which were not. There are exceptions, but it appears from the comparison exercise that the compiler has generally followed the practice of including non-fiction material which is not clearly identified as such in the magazines, and of omitting that which is. And from this it may be concluded that the bulk of all the entries derive from data given in tables of contents rather than from the entry-title pages themselves. Relying on those tables may expedite the compilation process, and is sometimes unavoidable, but doing so with any regularity places the indexer at the mercy of the one feature of the average magazine, in whatever genre, least celebrated for accuracy and reliability. Users, then, should be aware of the anomalous nature of the annotations in the CL and of the likelihood of encountering on occasion material indexed as fiction which will prove to be otherwise.

To summarize, the following table recaps statistically the results of the accuracy check of the two major sections:

```
Alphabetizing errors, IA: 95 x 2 (50% sample) =  190
Additional errors, IA:    19 x 2 (50% sample) =   38
Other errors, CL/IA:     106 x 10 (10% sample) = 1060
                                       Totals = 1288
```

As indicated above, care was taken to draw as representative a sample as possible, and certainly the 50% review given to the IA is likely to reflect accurately the approximate number of errors carried therein. There is no reason to think that the 10% review of the CL section is any less reliable as an indicator, but, assuming a sampling error in its favor of as much as 20%, the number to be found there could be as low as 850 or so. A downward adjustment reflecting this would produce a new over-all total of 1075.

Whether the number of errors to be found is 1075 or 1288 or some figure in between, the index would appear to carry an average of approximately one inaccuracy of one kind or another per page. This is a high incidence rate indeed for a reference work of this kind, and one which users will want to keep in mind as they use it to seek out data. Some of those inaccuracies are, of course, more significant than others, and the many that take the form of a simple and readily recognizable typo are likely to lead no one astray. But some kinds, such as omitted entries, misattributions, and incorrectly cited title entries, could on occasion prove troublesome. Certainly, those who rely on the work to draw up checklists for incorporation elsewhere will want to approach it cautiously.

We have in **Monthly Murders**, then, a reference work of major proportions, not without its faults and sometimes frustrating features, but one that breaks new ground in its field and offers aficionados of the mystery short story--a too long neglected component of the genre--a mass of useful data not heretofore catalogued. The tables of contents comprising the bulk of the "Chronological Listing" are in themselves of limited value to the average user, but collectors especially will appreciate the information that section provides about obscure magazines and the clarification offered therein of the frequently confusing dating practices employed by some publishing houses, obscure and otherwise. Avid readers will find the listings in the "Index by Author" of material help in tracking down unread stories by favorite writers, though the absence there of title change information will occasionally raise false hopes. And researchers too will have reason to welcome the appearance of the work, offering as it does the grist--of spotty reliability though some of it may be--for inquiries into the history and development of the genre's short story form and the careers of its practitioners. It is not the easiest kind of

[Continued on page 31]

The Fattest Man in the Medical Profession

Bob Sampson

Amid deafening self-applause, the February 7. 1925, issue of **Flynn's** announced a new short-story series by Anthony Wynne. Featuring Dr. Eustace Hailey, the "Harley Street Giant," the series would be

> a fund of pure, inductive reasoning of a type that seemed, unfortunately, to have been going out of style in detective literature. It is a cheering thing that the entrance of **Flynn's** into the field of detective literature has given rise to a new energy and a new spirit among creators of this type of story.

Flynn's was then about a year old, and at this early stage the magazine bubbled with English authors and English detectives and fiction that heaved massively onward through well-mannered crime among the wealthy. It was a peculiarly sedate beginning for one of the 1930s' prime publications for slug-and-shoot-'em fiction. But in 1925, even **Black Mask** slumbered. Whenever a pulp-paper magazine was able to feature a new English detective, they called out the drum and bugle corps.

In Dr. Hailey's case, such festivities were not entirely misdirected. He was one of the mainstream figures following Holmes and Thorndyke, about the third generation. Among the doctor-detectives of the 1920s, he was a significant figure. His generation included Dr. Reginald Fortune (who also appeared in **Flynn's**), Dr. Bentiron (from **Detective Story Magazine**), and Dr. Goodrich (of **Cosmopolitan**). All these gentlemen were also scientific detectives, among their other abilities—although precious little science niggled at their days.

Dr. Fortune is remembered today, while Dr. Goodrich and Dr. Hailey are not. These circumstances may elate those who believe Heaven's justice to be doled out in exact measure, although on a frivolously long term. In Dr. Hailey's case, there is some reason for his obscurity. He was never quite of the first rank. He was always an almost-celebrity, popular but not furiously so, sufficiently well known but not accorded spontaneous ovations. He was, however, quite popular enough to sell a novel a year (both British and American editions) for more than twenty years. Way back then in the 1920s, when the world brimmed with innocent light, Dr. Hailey stood massively on the mystery novel scene.

He was "believed to be the fattest man in the medical profession.... Somehow, Nature had compensated him for his great bulk by affording him the grace to wear it becomingly." He had "one of the kindest and most charming faces in the world."

And so he joins that distinguished list of famous fat men, including Mycroft Holmes, Dr. Fell, and Nero Wolfe. As a class, fat men are inclined to inactive contemplation. Not Hailey. Improbably enough, he is a man of action, forever swarming over walls, through hidden passages, up drain pipes.

It is not clear how a man of immense fatness can fly about so. It is easier to do in books than in size-62 trousers. Dr. Hailey is, by the way, excessively tall and possessed of a strength that would be exceptional in a professional strong man.

Certainly the weight tells on him. He naps after dinner. (Or perhaps it is because of the wine, for he has a sensitive palate.) Normally he moves at a gait best described as sluggish--"There was a slowness about the doctor's movements which suggested an ox browsing in rich pasturage." This unflattering comparison also mentions that his eyes are ox-dull, listless and indifferent. But they miss nothing.

His residence and professional chambers are at 22 Harley Street. They are presided over by the butler, Jenkins, nearly as fat as Hailey, himself. At this address the doctor practices medicine, specializing in mental diseases, by appointment only. (Amateur detecting seriously interferes with regular office hours.) Hailey pursues his profession "in a desultory sort of fashion. He was a man of independent means, a bachelor."

By those casual remarks we free our hero from the chains of making a living and amusing a wife. He can devote himself utterly to crime detection, his devouring joy.

It is not that piddling crime which fills the blotter down at the police station. No. The doctor's interests are restricted to the crime puzzle, that intricate winding of motive and desire common to fiction, if not reality--where the primary murder problem is who called whom a liar first.

Such rude crimes have their own appeal. But not to Dr. Hailey. He requires something to make the dull eye glint. Something complex and unobvious, requiring at least a pinch of snuff every ten minutes.

He carries a silver box of snuff and snorts that noxious medication shamelessly, in the antique way. No slovenly behind-the-lip addiction for him.

However amateur is Hailey's standing, Inspector Biles believes "that there was no detective at the Yard with greater powers of deduction and analysis than the doctor."

Inspector Biles is the official arm of the law for the series. Once Hailey treated him for a nervous breakdown, and their friendship grew. Biles is "a tall lean man whose eyes and mouth seemed to be very widely separated. This peculiarity ... gave him a cold, rather inhuman appearance, yet he was ... a good fellow, if a trifle severe in his point of view."

Severe with a tendency to fix tenaciously on the most likely suspect and most obvious solution. This is not to suggest that Biles is entirely the fool cop of fiction: "Biles' capacity as a detective was very great, perhaps supremely great ... (although) he lacked ... knowledge of the human mind in its nobler manifestations."

Of course, his business is not generally with the noble manifestations of the human mind. But we need not quibble.

In the United States, Dr. Hailey's adventures appeared from 1924 to 1950 in magazine serials and short stories and in books--a short-story collection and twenty-nine novels. This mass of fiction was written by Anthony Wynne, the pseudonym of Dr. Robert McNair Wilson

(1882-1963). Born in Glasgow, Wilson spent a lifetime as a doctor and surgeon, and his record is studded with such gleaming titles as:

—House Surgeon, Glasgow Western Infirmary;
—Editor, Oxford Medical Publications;
—Consulting Physician of Ministry of Pensions.

In parallel with these professional activities, he wrote forty or fifty books: a long series of biographies—several of these on Napoleon and his circle—and other volumes on medical subjects. As a hobby, he also wrote mysteries. You wonder how he found the time.

The magazine appearances of Dr. Hailey, as far as they have been traced, were in **Flynn's** from 1924 to 1927.[1] The 1924 magazine was a thick-bodied affair with a posed, photographic cover. It offered a mixture of serials, novelettes, and short stories and was seasoned by occasional crime articles in which the writer's imagination floated high above the fields of fact. The magazine's chief competitor at this time was Street & Smith's **Detective Story Magazine**, which was publishing as many crook stories as mysteries. To carve out a share of the market, **Flynn's** turned to such well-known English names and series as Freeman's Dr. Thorndyke, Wallace's J.G. Reeder, and Bailey's Mr. Fortune.

And Anthony Wynne's new detective, Dr. Hailey, who made his first appearance in **Flynn** in a six-part serial, "The Sign of Evil" (November 29, 1924, through January 3, 1925).

The serial explores, in methodical detail, the can of worms exposed after the murder and mutilation of Sir William Armand. The body has vanished entirely away, but Dr. Hailey reasons out its location. When the poor fellow is discovered, they find he has been stabbed through both eyes. And on the tree at the murder scene appears a charm against the evil eye.

Consternation.

Jack Derwick, fiance of Armand's daughter, Estelle, is arrested and tried for the murder.

His situation, hopeless enough, is complicated by an embezzling lawyer, who has spent it all on a glittering actress. Later, the lawyer confesses in court and flops over, full of poison.

Such revelations do not deter British justice. Derwick is found guilty, a decision which leaves Dr. Hailey bewildered, confused, and annoyed. For all the evidence leads one way and all his instincts lead another.

As usual, instincts win. At the very final last hour, Hailey goes flying down a new trail, dragging behind him a flutter of Scotland Yard men. Not only does the doctor prove Derwick innocent, but he also uncovers an astounding series of previously unsuspected murders by a mass killer of dedication.

This gentleman is a frequently insane justice figure—a real true justice figure, no less. He undertakes to detect and punish when authority fails. In this instance, he is punishing cruel fathers who are guilty of frustrating their daughters' love affairs.

Considering the nature of young girls, it's hard to understand how so many fathers survived.

Thus well launched, Hailey next appeared in a series of short stories. These were later collected as part of **Sinners Go Secretly** (1927) and are the most sprightly and interesting tales of the Hailey series. The first **Flynn's** story, "The Moveable Hands" (February 7, 1925), concerns the murder of a lovely society girl. She has been stabbed in an artist's apartment and on her throat is found A Significant Clue—a small green spot. It is the mark of a collar button.

From this evidence, Hailey penetrates an unusual masquerade. The girl is a two-faced criminal who has been stripping jewels from all the fine houses.

But who killed her, and where are the jewels?

A lie tells Hailey the first answer; the hands of a clock reveal the second.

"The House of Death" (March 14, 1925) is an improbable adventure, very busy. The search is on for the head of England's cocaine traffic. Hailey gets too close and is attacked by a radio-controlled airplane. Undaunted, he ignites a forested hillside and destroys the hideout, the Master Fiend, the works.

"The Lonely Skipper" (March 28, 1925) is a religious fanatic who returns as his own ghost, preparing to hand-grenade his own wife. At the last possible second, Dr. Hailey shoots him dead. It is surprising how many of these stories end violently. The sedate mystery abruptly turns crimson in the final pages, as action overwhelms the intellectual puzzle.

"The Death Moth" (April 25, 1925) is launched by a blackmailer. His impeccable business instincts lead him to murder people whose wills are in favor of the blackmailer's victims. He dies accidentally in Hailey's hands.

"The Double Thirteen" (four-part serial, September 5 through 26, 1925) contains one of those tangles you get when mono-filament line backs up. It buzzes with Russian refugees intriguing bloodily, as Russian refugees do. Cipher messages float about. And hypnotism. Dr. Hailey plunges into endless trouble because he has a certain susceptibility to blond girls with pink cheeks.

Through the heart of the novel our massive hero, dressed in a Falstaff costume, charges about night-time London. It is a diverting spectacle. In this rig he shadows a young man to a drunken revel and gets clobbered with a poker alongside his head.[2]

In less frothy moments, he solves a complex cipher and clambers up a ruined castle wall in time to shoot down the leering fiend.

The action of the July 9, 1927, short story, "The Telephone Man," is as concentrated as an Army fruit bar. It is a succession of crises, in true pulp style. Within an hour, Dr. Hailey faces a revolver, hits a spy with a shoe, detects an attempt to set fire to an apartment by a lense that concentrates sunlight, wrecks a fire engine, wrecks his car, and frustrates the theft of Naval plans.

During the grand finale, he plays a less than heroic role. He is stuck inside his wrecked automobile, puffing redly. The heroine must shoot the head spy, who is scampering away with the plans.

The stories, like failing marriages, blend the real world with melodrama. They begin like traditional puzzle pieces and end galloping across the hedgerows of Hell. Along the way, all sorts of wonderfully obsolete gimmicks are tossed in: death rays in "The Lost Ancestor" (October 24, 1925); secret panels and a concealed passageway to a mystic temple in "The Horseman of Death" (five-part serial, September 17 through October 15, 1927; this serial is packed tight with jealousy, drug addiction, double murder, and a gaggle of infantile people struggling for a rich inheritance; all this, and it still manages to be dull).

Other short stories are built around a specific location: a revolving stage in the October 10, 1925, story, "The Revolving Death"; a ski run in the October 31, 1925, entry, "The Heel of Achilles." These are in the fine old tradition of seeing an interesting place for a murder and then thinking up a story to go with the scene.

Occasionally the stories rise above this shallow trifling to more formal cases, solidly in the mainstream of the mystery problem. Such a story is "The Cyprian Bees," which was included in Ellery Queen's anthology, **101 Years' Entertainment**. It is one of Dr. Hailey's more business-like cases and assures him a modest pedestal in the hall of great detectives. But few of his adventures are so classical; most are bright little romps, interesting but spoiled by irrelevant racing about. They are much more beguiling, to the modern eye, than the novels.

Like the doctor, himself, the novels lumber massively along, full of interesting matter that is introduced without celerity and presented in a monotone. The novels are the literary equivalent of valium. Their plots are brutally complex, requiring a huge cast of characters to dart feverishly about the scene of the crime, dropping clues and picking them up again. Each character conceals a secret. After the crime, each dodges and evades and talks, talks, talks. As a result, each novel seems a thousand pages long, stuffed by endless conversations recorded to the ultimate subordinate clause. A gray droning suffuses the prose. Alibis are chewed and rechewed. Then, suddenly, action, a burst of movement for two pages or three. After which the narrative sags back into torpor, without color, without movement, a soothing hum, very relaxing.

The Hailey series falls into the classic period of the mainstream detective story, the scene being England, the detective being the brilliant amateur of those times. The stories are complicated puzzles, filled with easily remembered characters who move across stoutly English backgrounds, here and there flecked with stoutly English bloodstains.

It is the familiar 1920s mystery format, later developed more elaborately by John Dickson Carr, Margery Allingham, Agatha Christie, and other eminences.

But with this difference. These masters of the classic mystery concentrate on fairly realized people in clearly realized settings—or as realized as the writer's skill permits. Within these frames, murder is the great abnormality. The problem is almost always to determine who committed the crime and why. The solution depends on untangling skillfully tangled evidence that points to a single individual.

In other mystery forms, the emphasis is moved from the problem to the struggle between opposing characters, which is the characteristic of the mystery adventure story. While a mystery problem is often used, it is not the subject of the narrative but the device that ignites the action. Concurrently, there is an increased use of gadgets, devices, and such tried machinery of melodrama as trap doors, secret rooms, and passages dramatically concealed.

As many variations of these two forms exist as there are choruses to the **Tiger Rag**. Still, if you observe from a high enough peak, the two types are reasonably distinct.

Wynne's Dr. Hailey stories are a cross breeding of these two types of mysteries. In all the serials and most of the short stories, a specific problem is to be fathomed. This is done after a long series of adventures and physical dangers. In the course of the action, the innocent are always suspected and often arrested; Dr. Hailey is always hopelessly stumped; supernatural elements and impossible situations grin hatefully; semi-science-fictional devices buzz and hum. Unfortunately, so much time is spent manipulating situations and devices that there is no character development, and certainly no exploration of character.

The decals are given names and pasted down. The story swirls up around them.

Although the stories are carved from wood, their central situations are fascinating. In **The Silver Scale Mystery** (1931), supernatural horror accompanies tricky murder, and there is a killing device that couldn't quite work as it is said to. **The Case of the Gold Coins** (1934) offers us a dead man on an unmarked beach. **The Toll House Murder** (1935) varies this idea by providing a corpse in an automobile on an unmarked snowfield. **The Red Lady** (1935) shows how a man may be stabbed to death while standing alone facing an audience. And **Death of a Golfer** (1937) works an interesting variation on the idea by showing how you can be stabbed to death on the tee, although no one could possibly have done it.

To all these problems, Dr. Hailey eventually finds answers. He is a stronger and more interesting character than his own series. He is not just an athletic fat man, but functions, more seriously, as a modified justice figure. Although he works closely with the police, these official connections in no way impede his solitary adventures. He has the assurance that, at the end, the police will look blandly on his transgressions--which are many and violent.

No limit is placed on the number of corpses that he can find. Scotland Yard never questions his right to do so. Nor does the Yard challenge the dead men he creates. If he kills (almost always by accident), it is to preserve the English way of life. And with that justification, he moves ponderously through the series, a goblin on the side of virtue.

The 1925 world is sound and good. He does not quarrel with it. His thought is undarkened by those rude problems which occupied H.G. Wells and the Socialists. He is a protector of society, willing to see it improved, but not deeply modified. If he was aware of social faults, he never says so. He sees progress. He delights in man's inventions that lead, on a rising spiral, to new, cool beauty.

In a speeding car (Chapter XI, "The Double Thirteen"), he considers the situation of man:

> Speed of this exquisite impulsive kind thrilled him. It was, he told himself, the reward of science, of man's infinite labor against overwhelming odds, against darkness and doubt and superstition and weakness. He reflected that only knowledge, accurate observation and meticulous application is certain. The art of the detective is the art of civilization.

If only science were enough. If only civilization were less fragile. It was less than five years to economic collapse. It was less than fifteen to the Battle of Britain.

NOTES

[1] **Flynn's** altered its name every few years, becoming **Flynn's Weekly** (1925-1927), **Flynn's Weekly Detective Fiction** (1927-1928), and finally **Detective Fiction Weekly** (1928-1942). After purchase by Popular Publications, it was continued as **Flynn's Detective Fiction** (1943-1944) and **Detective Fiction** (1951).

²In the very next novel, **The Mystery of the Ashes** (1927), he again attends a fancy dress ball as Falstaff, again finds himself leaping like a gazelle over London rooftops.

The Anthony Wynne Mystery Novels

NOTE: The following novels are arranged in chronological order. Where significant title changes were made between British and American editions, both titles are given, together with, it is hoped, the first dates of publication for each. Title changes were frequent, depending on which side of the Atlantic you were reading on and which edition you had picked up. While most or all of these publications are assumed to feature Dr. Eustace Hailey, that fact has not been strictly confirmed in the case of three of the last four novels published--**The House on the Hard, Murder in the Church,** and **Death of a Shadow**--although it is likely that he appears in them as well. As usual, corrections and additions would be appreciated.

1925 **The Mystery of the Evil Eye** (U.S.: **The Sign of Evil**)
1926 **The Double Thirteen**
1927 **The Mystery of the Ashes**
1927 **Sinners Go Secretly** (short stories)
1928 **The Horseman of Death**
1928 **The Dagger**
1928 **The Red Scar**
1929 **The Room with the Iron Shutters**
1929 **The Fourth Finger**
1930 **The Blue Vesuvius**
1930 **The Yellow Crystal**
1931 **Murder of a Lady**
1931 **The Silver Arrow** (U.S.: **The White Arrow,** 1932)
1931 **The Silver Scale Mystery**
1932 **The Case of the Green Knife** (U.S.: **The Green Knife**)
1932 **The Case of the Red-Headed Girl** (U.S.: **The Cotswold Case,** 1933)
1933 **The Case of the Gold Coins**
1933 **The Loving Cup** (U.S.: **Death out of the Night**)
1934 **Death of a Banker**
1935 **The Toll House Murder**
1935 **The Red Lady**
1936 **Murder in Thin Air**
1937 **Murder in the Morning**
1937 **Death of a Golfer**
1938 **Death of a King** (U.S.: **Murder Calls Dr. Hailey**)
1939 **Door Nails Never Die**
1940 **The House on the Hard**
1941 **Emergency Exit**
1942 **Murder in the Church**
1950 **Death of a Shadow**

Deadly Edges of the Gay Blade

Martha Alderson

Perhaps the most notable characteristic of mystery novels is their reflection of present day topics, styles, and mores. We get a very clear picture of the speakeasies and the prohibition hysteria of the twenties, for example, from Dashiell Hammett. Some of us have at least some understanding of contemporary Wall Street through reading Emma Lathen's mysteries. It is not surprising, then, for there to be several mystery series in the seventies and eighties that have homosexuality as a topic by featuring homosexual detectives. Homosexuality is not new, but it does seem to be now in vogue.

This article discusses two series that feature gay sleuths. One series is by Nathan Aldyne and one is by Joseph Hansen. There are so far two Aldyne books: **Vermilion,** published in 1980; and **Cobalt,** published in 1982. There are six Hansens in the series under discussion. The first, **Fadeout,** was published in 1970, and the sixth, **Gravedigger,** was published in 1982.[1]

The moods and the personalities of the main characters in the two series are quite different. The Aldyne books are full of fun and colorful characters. The main character has a great sense of humor and is overtly gay, by both old and new definitions. The Hansen books are harder, with death and foul play pervading them from beginning to end. They fall in what might be called the "California Dick" group in the Chandler-Hammett-Macdonald tradition. The Hansen main character is, in his own words, "an aging homosexual" [**Gravedigger,** p. 22, and elsewhere] and has the worries of the world on his shoulders. There is a similarity, though, in the treatment of the characters in the two series, which is that, true to the mystery genre, the authors have great belief in the mental and physical superiority of their heroes.

If at least a secondary purpose of most mystery novels is to impart information about a special subject, both the Aldyne and the Hansen books meet the objective by presenting homosexuality as a life-style--both very different from and not so different from any other. Joseph Hansen comments about this theme:

> Homosexuals have commonly been treated shabbily in detective fiction--vilified, pitied, at best patronized. This was neither fair nor honest. When I sat down to write **Fadeout** in 1967, I wanted to write a good, compelling whodunit, but I also wanted to right some wrongs. Almost all the folksay about homosexuals is false. So I had some fun turning cliches and stereotypes on their head in that book.[2]

One tribute to Hansen's success is found in **Murder Ink**, wherein Solomon Hastings comments that "with Hansen the homosexual in crime fiction finally achieves three-dimensionality."[3]

In both the Aldyne and the Hansen series there are enough different types of characters to fit anyone's idea of a "typical" male homosexual. There are drag queens, muscle men, and swishy artists. But there are also gay strong, silent types; ruggedly handsome gay men; gay parents; and successful, non-flamboyant gay business executives.

In both the Hansen and the Aldyne novels, many plot complications arise from subjects common to all society, others from those peculiar to a homosexual counter culture. Scenes in gay bars and drag parties, the threat of blackmail, dangerous bitterness of closet homosexuals, for example, provide settings and motives in both series. A Provincetown costume party in Aldyne's **Cobalt** has scenes that provide clues for latter consideration. (The party theme is the Garden of Evil, and among the attending couples are Joan and Christina Crawford, Attila the Hun and Anita Bryant, and Ronald Reagan and John Hinckley.) In Aldyne's **Vermilion**, a not-so-straight detective haunts Boston's gay bars, both the classy private ones and the common working-class ones, looking for suspects in a murder case. In Hansen's **Fadeout** and also in **Gravedigger**, the hero solves the crimes after realizing that certain main characters or victims who are married men are in fact homosexual. In **Death Claims, Troublemaker,** and **The Man Everybody Was Afraid Of**, gay men have been falsely accused of murder. They all had possible motives and probable opportunity but were prime suspects largely because they were gay. The investigations are in gay bars, with loud media-prone gay activists, at gay talent shows and beauty contests, as well as in other more traditional settings. All of the books combine scenes and themes of homosexual specialties with more common events.

Nathan Aldyne has a team of two as amateur sleuths: Daniel Valentine, who is gay, and Clarisse Lovelace, who is not. Valentine's profile is more clearly drawn than Clarisse's, perhaps because readers might be expected to understand him less. Val is a young bartender in a gay bar in Boston, or, temporarily, in a gay bar in Provincetown. (Both Val and Clarisse have the opinion that almost all of Boston is gay, a rather startling generality. [**Vermilion**, p. 34] What would Robert B. Parker's Spencer think of that?) Val has been a social worker but was forced out of his job in a prison by a resentful corrupt politician whom Val had exposed. As a bartender, Val is, of course, still a social worker. What could be more natural? On the less serious side, Val is a playboy. A recurrent problem for him, in fact, is having lovers who want him full time. Sex, frequent and varied, is a predominant feature of his life. Val's non-sexual hobby is collecting playing cards, a not very interesting hobby which does not add to plot or subplot. Val's very active sex life, his fixation with old movies and movie stars, and his dull if not silly card collection would seem to combine to make Val a light-weight character, not to mention a kind of male homosexual stereotype. In spite of this, however, his image is a very positive one. Val is a happy and fulfilled person, sensitive and intelligent. He never seems to suffer from self-doubt and certainly never from embarrassment. He sees no reason to hide his sexuality. He is not himself given to extremes, but he is tolerant toward friends and acquaintances who are rather kinkier than he is. Val is perceptively suspicious of the self-righteous, with good reason as the plots develop. Physically, Val is, of course, handsome, healthy, and desirable. As Aldyne explains,

Valentine made a decent wage at the bar and consistently received generous tips—not just because he was efficient, which he was, nor simply because he was congenial and a good listener when the occasion warranted, which it often did, nor only because he was handsome and hot, but because of a smoothly balanced combination of all three of these elements. [**Cobalt**, p. 11]

Joseph Hansen's main character, Dave Brandstetter, is a very different sort of person from Daniel Valentine. Dave is an insurance investigator who deals with death claims in the mean streets and dusty roads around Los Angeles. He is good at his job. In **Skinflick** Dave's father's young widow Amanda says she knows of Dave's reputation as "the best in the business." [p. 37] In spite of his hard work and many successes with the insurance company his father owned, though, Dave was always very much aware that he was disliked by the other company powers because of his sexual preferences. Dave's explanation of why he stayed with the company until his father's death speaks of his convictions and his aptitude: "'My part was to play straight in a vicious game,' he said. 'I like it. I still do. That's why I'm not quitting. I'm one of the lucky people getting paid to do what I love to do.'" [**Skinflick**, p. 39]

Dave Brandstetter is a world-weary quintigenarian, but he carries his burdens gracefully. He is a man of good taste and refinement. Here is a typical description of one of his evenings at home: "While the martini chilled, he sliced tomato and avocado and laid the slices on lettuce on a plate. He tasted the martini, sighed, smiled, and switched on the radio. Brahms's **Liebeslieder** waltzes in the version for voices and piano. He sang along while he mixed a dressing." [**Gravedigger**, p. 111]

The plot structure is essentially the same in each of the Dave Brandstetter books: Brandstetter untiringly tracks witnesses and informants, collects data, follows intuitive leads, makes many false but honest trial accusations, and inevitably uncovers motives of psychosis or simple greed that have led to murder. Dave's life has changed tremendously through the series of novels. Each book presents a major crisis--the death of his lover of twenty years, the death of his father, serious problems in a new relationship, excitement and fears in another new relationship, a new house, a new car, a new closeness with Amanda Brandstetter. The Hansen books read first to last, then, present the complex saga of the ups and downs in the life of Dave Brandstetter. They can be read out of order with pleasure, but they are better in order, giving the reader the chance to ask at the end of each, "Will Dave Brandstetter ever find real happiness?"

Both Aldyne's Daniel Valentine and Hansen's Dave Brandstetter are handsome and strong. As such, they fit the mold of private eyes and amateur sleuths. Brandstetter, especially (in spite of his fifty-plus years by the sixth book!), can handle the obligatory violent scenes during which he suffers a normal number of concussions and broken ribs. Although Valentine has not been forced to prove his strength in the books so far, readers have no doubt that he could do so impressively. Partly these physical attributes make Val and Dave fit the mystery-hero traditions. But also, they seem designed to disprove the stereotype of the homosexual weakling. As part of this image building, Aldyne and Hansen both convince readers that their main characters are **not** perceived by the man or woman on the street as gay, an image they can choose to dispel when they wish. As Val and

Clarisse strolled arm in arm, their "appearance as a sterling couple of fashion and consequence was undermined only by Valentine's winking at every goodlooking man that passed." [**Cobalt,** p. 54] Val and Dave are "regular" types. "Real" men trust them, and "real" women desire them. On the other hand, by unknown signals (as well as by obvious winks), their sexuality is immediately recognized by gay men. In a review of **Gravedigger,** Walter Clemons accurately points out that "males many years his junior proposition [Brandstetter] as regularly as dames used to throw themselves at Philip Marlowe."[4] Although both Aldyne and Hansen write nonjudgmentally about more obvious gay types, they probably would never use any of them as heroes. This does represent a kind of stereotyping, too, but a publicly palatable one. The purpose of both authors is to break the assumption that all homosexuals are alike.

The use of these rugged gay heroes frees the authors to describe men with affectionate and realistic detail. John D. MacDonald, Alistair MacLean, or even Lillian O'Donnell or Ruth Rendell would not describe the sweet smiles, the loving expressions, the rippling muscles, or the shapely buttocks of men as attractively as do both Aldyne and Hansen. Dave Brandstetter meets a man with a "round, snub-nosed face. The hair above it had been dark and thick when he'd last seen it. Now it was gray and thin on a pink scalp. But the man still had boyishly rosy cheeks and blue eyes that were a little too gentle." [**Gravedigger,** p. 80] Another younger man's "tightly curled black hair was parted in the middle and combed over his ears. His brown eyes dreamed and his mouth was a dark rose. He could have posed for a Rossetti drawing. He could have been Rossetti, young, before the bloat set in." [**Death Claims,** p. 50]

Aldyne describes a man dressed as Polyphemus at the Garden of Evil party as one whose "shoulders were broad, his chest heavy with muscle beneath a mat of luxuriant tawny hair." [**Cobalt,** p. 14] In another description, Aldyne says that "Valentine ... had once thought Terry O'Sullivan handsome: a compact well-defined body, dark features, short curly black hair and a full black mustache." [**Cobalt,** p. 77]

These warm descriptions are not meant to be sensational. The writing style shows appreciation of men as whole human beings by viewing them in a liberated way which other writers could well take note of. The style is certainly refreshing.

The two Aldyne books and the six Hansen ones are enjoyable, credible mysteries. They are books with a message--that homosexual characters are not all comic or pathetic or evil. The message is not overbearing, though, and there is a balance of good and bad characters. The main characters in both series are attractive, humorous, and accomplished people. Dave Brandstetter and Daniel Valentine have very different styles. Let us hope they continue to sharpen their respective deadly edges--Brandstetter catching villains by being tough and suave, and Valentine swashbuckling his way through crime and injustice.

NOTES

[1] Two more Hansens in the Dave Brandstetter series are under contract with Holt, Rinehart and Winston for 1984 and 1985.

[2] **Twentieth-Century Crime and Mystery Writers,** edited by John M. Reilly (New York: St. Martin's Press, 1980), p. 727.

[3] Solomon Hastings, "Homosexuals in the Mystery: Victims or Victimized," **Murder Ink,** edited by Dilys Winn (New York: Workman, 1977), p. 495.

[4] Clemons, Walter, in **Newsweek,** 7 June 1982, p. 71.

Nathan Aldyne's
Daniel Valentine Mystery Novels

Vermilion. New York: Avon Books, 1980, 192 pp.

A male hustler has been murdered, and the murder may have been engineered by someone in Boston's gay community or possibly by a politician who is an avowed enemy of the gay community. Bartender Daniel Valentine and rental agent Clarisse Lovelace become involved in investigating the investigation and the murder.

Cobalt. New York: St. Martin's Press, 1982. Published in paperback by Avon Books, 1982, 201 pp.

Daniel Valentine is spending a fun-filled summer in Provincetown, Massachusetts, and has convinced Clarisse Lovelace to join him. Val, Clarisse, and their friends resent the several murders that interrupt the playful atmosphere, but they eventually solve the puzzles of the crimes.

Joseph Hansen's
Dave Brandstetter Mystery Novels

Fadeout. New York: Harper & Row, 1970. Published in paperback by Holt, Rinehart and Winston, 1980, 187 pp.

Dave Brandstetter, a death claims investigator for a Los Angeles insurance company in which his father is the major stockholder, is investigating the reported accidental death of a popular radio personality. Dave suspects attempted fraud and begins uncovering many sinister events in the lives of the people in the radio star's life.
In the midst of mourning for the death of the man who was his lover for twenty years, Dave finds a new romance, one of the suspects in the case.

Death Claims. New York: Harper & Row, 1973. Published in paperback by Holt, Rinehart and Winston, 1981, 166 pp.

The life insurance beneficiary would have changed from the

victim's son if the victim had lived another day. Dave Brandstetter starts his investigation with the obvious course of looking for the son. Dave discovers the son's reasons for hiding and his reasons for confessing to murder.

Dave's new romance is in trouble after only three months.

Troublemaker. New York: Harper & Row, 1975. Published in paperback by Holt, Rinehart and Winston, 1981, 155 pp.

A young co-owner of a gay bar has been killed. Dave finds numerous people with motives in addition to the young man everyone else thinks is guilty. Dave's investigation is in bars, parties, and homes of local homosexuals as well as the homes of the victim's relatives.

Dave's love life is not surviving the strains and requirements of Dave's job. Dave's aged father is critically ill.

The Man Everybody Was Afraid Of. New York: Holt, Rinehart and Winston, 1978. Published in paperback by Holt, Rinehart and Winston, 1981, 181 pp.

Dave investigates the death of a police chief who was a classic bigot but a popular police chief. The man accused is a gay activist who was especially disliked by the chief. During Dave's investigation, the chief's reputation as an upstanding citizen and fair law-enforcement agent crumbles.

Dave has broken up with his lover but still lives with him. There is a new lover who is serious about Dave but who is very young.

Skinflick. New York: Holt, Rinehart and Winston, 1979. Published in paperback by Holt, Rinehart and Winston, 1980, 194 pp.

A professed born-again Christian vigilante has been murdered. Police have arrested the owner of a pornographic book store because he had been a particular target of the victim's vigilante group. Dave discovers that judgments about righteousness cannot be made on the basis of appearances.

Immediately after his father's death, Dave left the insurance company where he had worked for many years. He now works for another company. He persuaded his father's widow to decorate a new house for him. Dave now lives alone, and his loneliness is only occasionally relieved by a passing fling.

Gravedigger. New York: Holt, Rinehart and Winston, 1982, 183 pp.

Once again Dave suspects a fraudulent life-insurance claim, this time for a teenaged girl. Dave has trouble finding not only the girl but also her father, who placed the claim. Dave meets adults who are afraid to be honest and then a psychopathic killer.

Dave is pursued by and eventually accepts a new lover. There are potential problems, but Dave seems satisfied. Dave has taken on responsibility for the mental health of his father's widow, and their new relationship is close.

REEL MURDERS
MOVIE REVIEWS
by Walter Albert

The University of Pittsburgh recently hosted the annual meeting of the Society for Cinema Studies and more than 150 scholars spent four very busy days delivering and listening to papers, attending film showings, and socializing. There were twenty-nine panels, each of them consisting of the reading of three or four papers, followed by discussions, and there was a variety of screenings, highlighted by Robert Altman's 1982 film, **Come Back to the 5 and Dime, Jimmy Dean, Jimmy Dean,** which the director attended for a post-screening session at which he responded to questions from a large and very sympathetic audience.

The general topic of the convention was film genre, and the often sparsely attended screenings--film scholars seem to prefer to talk and be talked at rather than cluster anonymously in improvised screening rooms--featured a series of films "on, in, and beyond the genre." Since the films were scheduled at the same time as the panels, I was constantly faced with agonizing decisions. However, I was able to reconcile most of my warring interests and managed to spend several hours in the dark watching Frank Borzage's **Mannequin** (1938), a "melodrama of fashion and fetishism with Joan Crawford"; Dario Argento's stylish horror film, **Suspiria** (1977); Robert Altman's very individual and probably unclassifiable comedy drama, **Brewster McCloud** (1970); and Max Ophuls' 1949 movie, **The Reckless Moment,** in addition to the festival screening of Altman's **Jimmy Dean** film. Since I had already seen DeMille's **Unconquered** (1947), Cassavetes' **Gloria** (1980), and William Richert's **Winter Kills** (1979), I managed a fairly comprehensive coverage of the convention films.

One of the things that was clear from several of the panels I attended was that there is increasing recognition of the fact that the sub-genres (musical, western, science-fiction, **film noir**) are not always "pure" and there is a fair amount of "bleeding" among the various types, with, for example, elements of the crime film or **film noir** turning up in westerns or in musicals. Since writers on film have traditionally had difficulty defining **film noir,** establishing firm chronologies, and identifying those films which are undeniably **noir,** this makes it possible to examine a wide range of films in a number of different categories. Anyone who has looked very closely at the two major books on **film noir,** the Silver/Ward **Film Noir: An Encyclopedic Reference to the American Style** (Overlook Press, 1980) and Foster Hirsch's work, **The Dark Side of the Screen: Film Noir** (A.S. Barnes, 1981), will have been struck by the lack of agreement on the basic body of films thought to constitute the official canon. There is, thus, under way what could be a very fruitful re-examination of the subject, and I would expect that over the next few years there will be major reformulations that will both define more precisely **noir** elements and refine their applications to particular films.

While both Silver/Ward and Hirsch list Max Ophuls' **Reckless Moment** in their filmographies, Silver/Ward point out the anomaly of casting a woman as the potentially doomed victim, rather than, as is usually the case in **noir** films, the tracked male. The casting is also ironic in that the woman is played by Joan Bennett, who was the destructive femme fatale in Fritz Lang's **Woman in the Window**, here playing an upper middle-class housewife who embarks upon a sequence of lies and deceptions to protect her daughter whom she mistakenly believes to be responsible for the death of her blackmailing lover. The film is based on a story by Elisabeth Sanxay Holding, "The Blank Wall," and has all the elements of standard woman-in-peril magazine fiction but reshaped by the superb direction of Ophuls into a subtle study of middle-class morality threatened by a seductive outsider (Shepperd Strudwick) who is "removed" and then replaced by an even more potentially dangerous threat (a blackmailer, James Mason, working with a totally unprincipled partner). The strength of the film is not only in the fluid, accomplished camera work which tracks Bennett in her increasingly more frantic quest for salvation and liberation, but in the bond which develops between Mason and Bennett, the rootless outsider, the black sheep, as he tells her, of his family, and the mother whose only concern is to protect her daughter from the consequences of her folly and keep the stain from contaminating the house and the other members of the family.

The film is at its most intense and claustrophobic (she is, after all, walled in by her fears and assumptions) in its handling of the interior spaces of the Harper house. Bennett paces incessantly through the house, nervously chain-smoking, trying to hide her machinations from her family, as if she were turning in a cage. In the foreground, the camera is most obsessive about Bennett's every move, but it is also recording, in the background, the routine of the family, so that the spectator is bound by a sense of a precarious balance between the two levels and of the constant threat of the possibility of the rupturing of the fragile membrane that separates the two. Bennett plays the role with a dark distraction in which she seems always to be just a bit to one side of the on-screen action, plotting her next move. She is frequently interrupted, never really alone--even when she is driving with Donnelly, the character played by Mason, at a traffic light someone leans from the next car to talk to her. She is always tracked by the camera, but this is symptomatic of a larger trajectory at which her every movement seems to coincide with an intersection. There is no one moment in the film that is in itself irretrievably reckless. It is rather the narrative, restlessly exploring the implications of movements, that is reckless. Lucia Harper (Bennett) can only be saved by the intervention of an outside agency, initially threatening, finally converted into something benign and protective, a member of her extended family taking from her the role she cannot herself carry off successfully and restoring her as manager of the household and bearer of the telephone message to a no longer threatening exterior world, "Everything's fine."

There are some of the recognizable features of **film noir** in the depiction of the doomed character (here uncharacteristically rescued), in the menacing shadows and reflections, and in the atmospheric--and sometimes sordid--milieux that we associate with the genre. But **The Reckless Moment** is no more to be restricted by a characterization of genre than any other film that uses form not for constriction but for expansion and elaboration. This is probably not a film of the same distinction as Ophuls' **Pleasure, The Earrings of Madame X,** and **Lola Montes,** but it is a film of uncommon intelligence and taste, transforming its materials into something at once imperious and elusive, a perfect demonstration of Ophuls' belief that, in art, "the most insignificant, the most unobtrusive among [details] are often the most evocative, characteristic and even decisive. Exact details, an artful little nothing, make art."

[Continued from page 15]
index to work with, especially on a sustained basis (the regrettable absence of issue date information in the "Index by Author" will more often than not slow the user to a crawl), and it is not inexpensive either. But as the only work if its kind yet to appear, it is at once indispensible to the serious student.

[Continued from page 42]
it should have been told at all. The problem is not with the downfall of Eddy Sachs, but with the basic nature of suspense writing. Van de Wetering's commitment to the Zen principle that the ultimate meaning is nothingness, which conditions everything he writes, affects the resolution of **The Butterfly Hunter** in a way that is unusual and surprising, but it may be disappointing to the reader who expects the normal satisfactions provided by writers like Ken Follett and Frederick Forsyth. The reader may not object to being tricked or even conned, as we frequently are by a suspense writer, but he will probably want to come out of a 200-page novel with something more than a handful of nothing. (George N. Dove)

VERDICTS Book Reviews

Jon L. Breen. **Listen for the Click.** Walker & Co., 1983, 173 pp., $12.95.

There is a kind of detective novel set in a world of quiet gentility, a magical place without pain or grief or terror, a place where corpses don't bleed and the emotions of the living are always under iron control. During the lulls in the plot a Nice Young Man and Nice Young Woman get together, and in the final chapter, preferably at a ritual gathering of the suspects, the Brilliant Detective effortlessly exposes the murderer. The current generic name for a book of this sort is the English Cozy, because there's a myth that it's always been the exclusive property of British writers. In fact, however, a number of well-known Americans too have specialized in it, and Earl Derr Biggers' half dozen Charlie Chan novels (1925-1932) are models of the form.

Jon L. Breen, an award-winning mystery reviewer, short-story writer, and Biggers devotee, has set his first detective novel on this turf. Amid an unobtrusive but knowingly sketched background of Southern California's racing community, a jockey who had given many people potential murder motives is shot out of the saddle of a bronze horse statue on the lawn of a wealthy racing enthusiast's widow. The nephew of this dotty and whodunit-fixated old lady is racetrack announcer Jerry Brogan, whom Breen casts in the dual role of Nice Young Man and Clever Amateur Sleuth: if he wasn't sleeping with his Chicana girlfriend without benefit of a marriage license, he might have stepped straight out of a Biggers novel of the 1920s. Meanwhile, a suave con man and a shady private eye with literary ambitions launch a scheme to make Jerry's aunt believe that they're the Holmes and Watson of the west coast. In due course, after the underdog horse wins the big race, a Gathering of Suspects is arranged in the purest Charlie Chan movie tradition--"The murderer is in this room," one of the small army of detective figures in the book intones solemnly--and all the clues are put in order.

Breen combines quiet charm, gentle digs at several types of crime fiction, and a puzzle complete with such original touches as an over-obvious Big Secret that mutates into a huge joke and a clue hidden in the book's title. It's no Secretariat, but lovers of the soft-spoken whodunit will have a fine canter around the track with this thoroughbred. (Francis M. Nevins, Jr.)

Dick Francis. **Banker**. Putnam's, 1982.

Dick Francis began as a good writer, has honed his skills steadily and successfully, and is now—no question about it—simply, reliably, steadily excellent. **Banker** lives up to all expectations. In this tale of yet another side of racing, protagonist Tim Ekaterin, an upwardly mobile merchant banker, takes a flyer by recommending that his firm help to finance a stud farm whose owner wishes to buy a new stallion, Sandcastle. If the project works, and all the signs forecast success, the horse breeder will move well forward among his peers, Tim will affirm his place in the upper echelons of his bank, and Sandcastle will live a long, happy, profitable life. Everyone stands to gain—until many of Sandcastle's first batch of colts turn out to be deformed, and murder intrudes among the green pastures and white fences of the stud farm.

Tim undertakes to discover why these tragedies are occurring, intending both to protect the banks' investment and to aid Oliver Knowles, his newly made friend, new owner of Sandcastle. Both men pay a high price for justice, however—Oliver suffers an irreparable loss, and Tim undergoes the usual physical punishment Francis metes out to his heroes as well as losing some of the innocence and trust he has improbably but convincingly maintained into his early thirties.

Indeed, loss of innocence is a constantly present theme in this novel, which is a serious study of good and evil. Two marvelous portraits of adolescents underscore it and serve to illuminate the portrait of Tim. The stud farm is clearly symbolically Edenic, as is, surprisingly but also convincingly, the bank. The serpents in both locations have that blind spot of irresponsibility on which crime writers so frequently (and so fairly and so truthfully) capitalize. None of the nuances, however, does one thing, even momentarily, to dull the interest or quell the suspense of this fine novel—just note, for instance, the riveting first scene.

Impatient readers may remark that **Banker** gets off to a slow start, but that quibble is really invalid. The financial scheme in question is an extended one, taking several years to come into full fruition, so the tempo is appropriate and effective—it worked in Christie's **Death on the Nile**, and so it should, and does, work here. Out of the gate and down the stretch, **Banker** is a winner. (Jane S. Bakerman)

P.D. James. **The Skull Beneath the Skin.** Charles Scribner's Sons, 1982, 328 pp.

P.D. James's private investigator, Cordelia Gray, is back in action again in the second novel devoted to her adventures, **The Skull Beneath the Skin**. This time, she's off to Courcy Island, a couple of miles off the Dorset coast, to protect actress Clarissa Lisle, Lady Ralston, who had been receiving death threats. Courcy is the family seat of novelist Ambrose Borringe, who takes pleasure in all things Victorian and perhaps particular pleasure—or at least interest—in the restoration of the little theater his great-grandfather originally built for the delectation of his houseguests, particularly the Prince of Wales and Lillie Langrty. Lady Ralston is to star in a production in the Courcy theater.

Cordelia's fellow guests are an interesting if disquieting lot, and when murder intrudes, as it will during English house parties, they are, of course, the only suspects. In that way, **The Skull Beneath the Skin** is a traditional closed-circle crime novel, the form James prefers because of her interest in the impact of tragedy upon the people most directly involved and in the duality of impulse within those folk: to help locate and expel the killer and to protect their privacy, their own secrets, their own circle. Also in the tradition of some of her fictional predecessors, perhaps Marple and Poirot particularly, Cordelia once again takes the law into her own hands and both withholds information from the police and determines to force them into action they may well be reluctant to undertake. James leaves little doubt in her readers' minds that her young detective will succeed in manipulating the cops—just as she did in her first outing, **An Unsuitable Job for a Woman.**

These traditional elements are not, however, the only allusions with which James plays in **The Skull Beneath the Skin.** Fans will be reminded instantly of Michael Innes's **Hamlet, Revenge!**, for the situation—the revival of an old play with a toney crew of players and audience members—is the same. Because of the island setting and the steady (though severely limited) decimation of characters, readers will also be reminded of Christie's **And Then There Were None** (aka **Ten Little Niggers** and **Ten Little Indians**). And a key motivation-for-suspects device, the idea of old, nearly forgotten crimes coming back to haunt present characters, will call to mind a host of other mysteries as well as, again, **And Then There Were None.** James is so poised, so skillful, that one can be sure that these allusions are intended, and, for the most part, they are successful.

Riskier but also successful here are James's echoes of her own work. As in **An Unsuitable Job for a Woman,** she introduces a young man of great sensitivity, great capacity for introspection and suffering, who cannot come to terms with the terrors and pressures of the "real" world; that worked earlier, and it works here. And Cordelia's fetish, the belt which once belonged to the victim in **An Unsuitable Job for a Woman,** is again an important feature in the new novel; keep an eye on it. It looks as if it will turn up yet again, one hopes not **too** regularly, if the Gray books become a long-lived series.

Certainly, Cordelia Gray is worth a series; her impulses are a fine combination of a quiet rage for true justice and the practicality which keeps her marginal business alive. Cordelia meets interesting if not always appealing people, and she is building a kind of extended family at work, having acquired a loyal, mildly intriguing office staff with two oddballs. Taken all in all, **The Skull Beneath the Skin** is worthy of James's standards, largely because of the sense of evil she evokes and because the guts and poise needed to withstand that menace are inherent in Cordelia Gray. She needs them to survive country house life. (Jane S. Bakerman)

Ellery Queen. **The King Is Dead.** Little, Brown, 1952.

The King Is Dead is a curious book. One of the major Queen charms is that even the Queen dying message formula is handled so originally whenever it recurs that one is hardly aware he is reading a formula book. Originality is the Queen trademark, far more so than with any other writer of the polite school.

Yet that pre-eminence among polite mystery writers rules out certain things that many a reader finds appealing in other writers' work. Even in a realistic vein, Queen books never approach the gritty realism (perhaps even naturalism) that is the trademark of the hardboiled writers. And, of course, Queen **never** wrote the pulp sort of mystery, not even in those paperback originals ghosted by various other hands.

The King Is Dead comes rather close to the pulp tradition, closer than we'd any right to expect, and it was written early enough to be almost certainly the work of Dannay and Lee. Imagine a super successful industrialist with a Howard Hughesish air of mystery and seclusiveness about him, shot in a locked room that is really a vault. Imagine a presidential request (and it would have come from that glorious old commoner, Harry S, in those days) that the Queens serve as a sort of special-agent-of-the-president investigators, right spang in the tradition of the Ed Noon of the seventies, the "Presidential Agent" series by Joseph Milton of the sixties, and Lanny Budd of the forties (whose final adventure appeared the year after **The King Is Dead**). Imagine secret, private research (with the researcher held as a slave by the wicked arms manufacturer—straight out of the thirties pulps) that would have proliferated the atomic bomb among dozens of irresponsible governments (is there a responsible one?), just as the political wisdom of the great powers has since accomplished—and the reality is every bit as frightening as the thought of it was in the early fifties. Imagine a fiercely protective private security force that behaves like a minimized Gestapo. Imagine two brothers for "the King," one a business genius who is the power behind the throne, and the other a miserable alcoholic whose one goal is to destroy the megalomaniac brother. Imagine a wife who is a non-funny version of the character played by Eva Gabor in TV's **Green Acres**. Quite a mix, and Dannay and Lee even manage to make it (momentarily) convincing.

The solution to the shooting is Queenishly ingenious. The solution to the tangled relationships is satisfactory. And the bringing down of the wicked armsman's empire is eminently satisfying.

Queen readers expect to be surprised. But this book exceeds one's ordinary expectations. Read it and see for yourself. (Jeff Banks)

J.S. Borthwick. **The Case of the Hook-Billed Kites**. St. Martin's Press, 1982.

The tale of detection based on accurate knowledge of some specialized field (orchid growing, horse racing, Wall Street finance) has always had a particular fascination for the mystery lover. In her first novel, J.S. Borthwick has achieved a happy combination of her acquaintance with birdwatching and birdwatchers and a strong feel for time, place, and the current concerns of the reading public. Although she invents the Dona Clara National Wildlife Refuge and the town of Boyden, Texas, which together comprise the scene of most of the major events in her story, she locates them on the Rio Grande, between the real cities of McAllen and Harlingen, and her chapter-headings are exact calendar dates. The rest of the feel of immediacy is supplied by such topical concerns as the border drug traffic problem, the ever-present encroachment of illegal aliens, and even a Laetrille-like cancer treatment called Celluwell.

The author knows her birds and is not a stranger to those of the Rio Grande Valley. The hook-billed kite is nigh to impossible here, but it is just the malevolent-looking creature to furnish the major clue in the plot. Here are the "spectaculars," the specialties of the area, such as the kiskadee and the green jay, the black-bellied whistling duck and the rose-throated becard. Swallow-tailed kites are seen from vans (she calls them minibuses); the paraques and screech owls call at night, and the colorful Blackburnian warbler can wander into this area.

Borthwick handles the equipment of the mystery with satisfactory skill, to the extent that all of the major suspects are deprived of alibis, and suspicion is moved from one to another in such fashion as to hold the suspense at a reasonable pitch. Clues range from an old standby (the time of a rain shower as a key to the time of a murder) to a highly imaginative use of the birdwatcher's familiar field card in the perpetration of a crime. The author plays strictly fair, supplying a clue which the knowledgeable birdwatcher should be able to spot a good seventy pages ahead of the uninformed amateur. Contrary to the publisher's blurb, there is no "thoroughly delightful and intrepid amateur detective" for this mystery, which is really solved as a result of the joint efforts of two moderately gifted amateurs and one competent policeman. The reader with a strong sense for plot development may experience some annoyance with the fact that Borthwick permits her mystery to be solved fairly early and then strings out her story with a chase prolonged beyond what the events have justified, including a cliff-hanger that is almost painfully literal.

In addition to her birds, the author also knows her people: the professional ornithologist and the botanist; the tour guides, good and bad, ethical and unethical; the arrogant teen-ager who knows birds in and out but nothing else; the dedicated birder; the simple or novice birdwatcher; the inappropriately dressed clothes-horse and skirt-wearer; the unsophisticated feeder-watcher who informs an expert birder she wishes he could see **her** cardinals; and the native Texans who neither know nor care what comes in their area in feathers or petals. As for her individuals, Borthwick knows how to make them come alive with a quick brilliant touch. Thus Cheryl Cabot, the buxom motel clerk, has a simple rule regarding dress: if it fits, it is too big. Mrs. Axminster in her dirndl looks "like a bed pillow tied in the middle," and the tour leader, Major Foster, fresh among his early-morning followers, is "moving in a cloud of aftershave lotion."

The Case of the Hook-Billed Kites is a book that is likely to appeal to people on all levels of expertise, though a little less quoting of zoological names (called species names in the novel) might have made the average reader a little more comfortable with the story. (George and Helenhill Dove)

Leslie McFarlane. **Ghost of the Hardy Boys: An Autobiography.** Methuen/Two Continents, 1976.

Since most autobiographies I read turn out to be as interesting as watching your neighbor's home movies (the lightweight and bland **Agatha Christie: An Autobiography** comes immediately to mind), I approached this book with a great deal of reservation. My fears were unfounded; this is a good book.

Leslie McFarlane gives us a writer's view of how it was to grind out manuscripts for a fiction factory during his career working for the Stratemeyer Syndicate. From ghost writing Dave Fearless to the Hardy Boys for a set fee and no rights, he explains the pros and cons of hack writing as he rehashes one stirring juvenile saga after another.

Born in the Canadian mining region of Ottawa Valley at the turn of the century, McFarlane gives us an informative and well-detailed description of what it was like to live in the wild mining towns, with their own special codes, laws, and ethics. This section provides an excellent bit of reference and history on an area and time that is not too often written about.

McFarlane cut his writing teeth on small newspapers throughout this region and eventually ended up working for a ruthless publisher who took delight in putting other papers out of business and shafting his own employees in the name of free enterprise. McFarlane pulls no punches in giving a first rate account of what it was like working for this bastard (McFarlane's own description of the man) and being a reporter on small regional newspapers.

This book is must reading for anybody interested in writing, because of the straightforward way McFarlane explains his experiences in the various fields of writing he worked. You'll read things in here you won't find in any of the writing books.

For mystery collectors the book contains no bibliography of McFarlane's work nor does it have an index. Unusual, but not unheard of in an autobiography. Even so, it may be a good item for your collection.

Pleasurable reading. (Randy Himmel)

Ron Goulart. **Big Bang**. DAW, 1982, 160 pp., $2.25.

If you go by the odds, they're over a thousand to one that you'll find this latest work by Ron Goulart, a wacky wordsmith in the tradition of no one but himself, over in the science fiction of your favorite B. Dalton Bookstore, and not in with the mysteries at all. If it were to come down to it, I guess that's where I'd put it, too, but if you care for your detective-story reading served to you a la a combination of Craig Rice and Crazy Guggenheim, why not step across an aisle or two and give yourself a real treat?

The proprietors of Odd Jobs, Inc., are Jake and Hildy Pace, who are assisted at times by their tipsy attorney, John J. Pilgrim, and an electronic eavesdropper named Steranko. Their specialties are cases "normal agencies won't go near, cases even our government has given up on." The year is 2003, in case you were wondering, and the President are a pair of Siamese twins named Ike and Mike, joined together at the funny bone.

The case is a fairly ordinary one, all things considered: a series of huge explosions is wiping out important world figures, as well as anyone else in the general vicinity. The Paces suspect stock manipulators at work, rather than your standard, every-day sort of terrorist type of person.

Rex Sackler, Luther McGavock, Ed Jenkins, and Race Williams (among others) have already failed on the case. (Goulart is a notorious name-dropper, isn't he?)

His work is also filled with hilariously funny glimpses into today's media-conscious society, stirred up thoroughly and served here as a fast-paced (extremely), no-nonsense (well, maybe just a little) detective novel. I mean, what other mystery story have you read recently that requires the use of a Captain Texas secret decoder device as an **essential** part of the solution? [B] (Steve Lewis)

Bill Pronzini. **Scattershot**. St. Martin's, 1982, 172 pp., $10.95.

Business, as they say, is booming. For Bill Pronzini's pulp-collecting detective, for one, and for readers of private-eye fiction, for hundred, if not thousands of others.

Doomsayers to the contrary, the p.i. story is alive and--would you believe?--**thriving**. I've got a pile here you wouldn't believe, and if I weren't awfully careful about it, I could read nothing but.

Not that I would. I'd be burned out within a month if I did. I need a Leslie Ford every now and then, just to keep a proper perspective on things.

But back to "Nameless," as he has more or less officially been dubbed. All of a sudden he has more cases than he needs, especially just as his love life with Kerry (the lady he hit it off with so well in **Hoodwink**) is turning sour.

Strangely enough, so do each of the three cases recorded in this book. Each becomes an "impossible" crime: a locked-room murder, a man who vanishes out of a constantly watched car, a wedding present that disappears out of a constantly guarded room.

Terrific stuff, but 100 percent guaranteed to produce ulcers for the detective that's supposed to solve them, or else—lose his license? Nah, it couldn't be ... could it? Life's never this rotten .... Is it?

People not in the know constantly confuse p.i. fiction with hard-boiled fiction. There is a relation, but nothing could really be much further from the truth. "Nameless" tries—he's a man, and he has a macho image to maintain, whether consciously or not—but he's also too soft and vulnerable. And likeable. He'd be hell to live with, but Kerry will come back. Won't she?

Hey, Bill! How long will we have to wait for the next one? [A minus] (Steve Lewis)

Charles Merrill Smith. **Reverend Randollph and the Holy Terror**. Avon, 1982 [first published in 1980], 236 pp., $2.50.

From the inner working of crematoria (two books back) to an intimate, close-up look at life inside modern-day liberal Protestantism. It's quite a jump, but, if anything, it's certainly indicative of the widely varied kinds of background it is possible to find in the world of mystery fiction. (As if any of you reading this ever really doubted it.)

Changes are going on in this series, and many of them are of such a permanent nature that—is it possible?—this also marks the end of Rev. Randollph's career as a crime-solver.

In this, his fourth adventure—all of them reprinted now by Avon—not only does he finally marry his agnostic lady friend, local TV personality Samantha Stack, but after a year's tryout he is also installed as the permanent pastor of Chicago's wealthy Church of the Good Shepherd (denomination unspecified). By story's end he seems to be openly settling down, into a quiet, comfortable life where murder seldom intrudes—luckily for him, but in many ways a shame. Even though "Con" Randollph is ever only so-so as a detective, his warm, outgoing personality was always a most definite asset in all the cases he helped solve.

If this does turn out to be his final appearance, however, he does go out with a bang. A psychotic, poetic killer is stalking the priests and pastors of Chicago, and Randollph is warned that he is very high on the list of the killer's victims.

Among other matters, Randollph also finds he must defend himself against an attack by the local chapter of the Citizens for a Moral America. The issue is pornography, and, while the great TV debate is, of course, a side issue to the mystery at hand, it is one just as central to the series as a whole, bringing to bear as it does such crucial matters of character, and an overall outspokenly positive outlook on life. [B plus] (Steve Lewis)

John Gardner. **Icebreaker.** G.P. Putman's Sons, 1983, 301 pp., $10.95.

After a somewhat shaky start in **License Renewed,** James Bond (formerly agent 007) was off to a flying come-back in the second of John Gardner's pastiches of Ian Fleming's series, **For Special Services.**

In the third of the new series we find Bond up against a group of neo-Nazis located on the Soviet-Finnish border. How he foils them is in the best Bond tradition of yore. This is far and away the strongest book of the three.

One can almost feel the cinematic possibilities of this book. No doubt that was in Gardner's mind as he wrote. After all, how many more of the originals are left for Roger More, Sean Connery, et al?

Pastiche is difficult to pull off. Gardner really does so, but there is a lot of his own style mixed in with the imitation Fleming. It maintains a steady balance that makes for a fast-paced book with lots of twists and turns before the ending.

You can almost forget that Bond was a child of the fifties, for he feels right at home in the eighties. He exhibits all the trademark hardware (sleek customized car, electronic gadgetry, etc.) that we have come to expect, as well as the beautiful women that he is forever entangled with (we should all have his problems!).

All in all, this is a fun book. Excitement, escapism, and sex, and all in good taste! What could be better? (Alan S. Mosier)

Robert B. Parker. **The Widening Gyre.** Delacorte, 1983, 183 pp., $12.95.

In his tenth book about the classiest hardnosed detective ever to appear in print, Robert B,. Parker has only re-affirmed my earlier conclusions as to the real identity of Spenser.

Spenser is Parker; Parker is Spenser. It is Parker's code that is embodied in the character of Spenser.

Spenser has most often been compared to John D. MacDonald's Travis McGee, and with good reason. Spenser is quite similar except in the aspect of his being a one-woman man. Thereby hangs this tale.

I felt that **Ceremony** (Parker-Spenser's last outing) was a rehash of earlier plot twists and character devices, and so to some extent is **The Widening Gyre.** But there is a difference in the inclusion of the subplot, and an over-all difference in tone. Parker has Spenser back on the track and in excellent shape.

Spenser has lost Susan Silverman to her new occupation in Washington, D.D., and he does not know what to do or feel about it. This book is almost equally about Spenser's coming to grips with his personal life as well as his battle to free a senatorial candidate from blackmail.

Being from Boston, I always enjoy reading about the familiar names and locations that Parker liberally disperses throughout his books. Parker's usual cast is here, too; the delectable Susan, his Marvin Haglerish associate Hawk, State Police officer Martin Quirk, and Spenser's surrogate son Paul Giacomin, and a local Boston heavy, the neanderthal Joe Broz.

As usual, this is a tightly written, fast-paced book. It is a pleasure to find a literate writer working in the mystery trade. Although I felt less than satisfied with **Ceremony, The Widening Gyre** is the best Spenser effort since **Early Autumn.** Welcome back, Robert B. Parker. (Alan S. Mosier)

Bill Pronzini. **Undercurrent**. Random House, 1973, 213 pp.

Young, recently married, vulnerable Judith Paige comes to Pronzini's private detective character with a suspicion that her husband is seeing another woman. He doesn't like this type of work, but he needs the money and agrees to investigate. The husband gets murdered and Nameless (so called by critics and reviewers because Pronzini doesn't tell you his name in any of the books) feels obliged to investigate. The more he digs, the more complex the case gets.

The book, indeed the series, is well written with believable characters. Pronzini reserves some clues, but not enough or so blatantly that the reader wants to cry "No fair." A minor fault is the use of details from previous cases. Although this does serve to make Nameless more real, it pulls some punches if you read the books out of sequence and is downright frustrating if you can't obtain some of the books. Overall, well worth reading. (Linda Toole)

Richard Putrill. **Murdercon**. Doubleday, 1982, 181 pp., $10.95.

The jacket says Doubleday Science Fiction, but this is really murder at a sci-fi con. You ought to be able to spot who and why in the first dozen pages (If I did, anyone can) but there are a few intriguing items. (In case you are comatose, the author tells you who and why around page 80.) The characters are interestingly drawn, and there are some nice touches about San Diego. Not at all challenging, it's a nice book to read if you've got a cold or the flu--you don't have to work at it, but it's interesting enough to take your mind off your troubles. (Linda Toole)

Peter Nusser. **Der Kriminalroman** [The Detective Novel] (Sammlung Metzler M 191). Stuttgart, Germany: Metzler, 1980, viii, 186 pp.

Here is a serious, systematic, academic study of the detective novel. Included are chapters on "the method of investigation," the structure and history of the detective novel, and the "psycho-sociological explanations" of the detective novel's effects on its readers. Nusser maintains throughout a sharp distinction between the detective novel and the thriller, where he places the hardboiled novels. In the chapter on the method of investigation he makes further distinctions, with crime literature being the general category which includes thrillers, criminal literature (Dostoyevsky's **Crime and Punishment**), criminal adventure stories, spy novels, and detective stories proper. Unfortunately, other than **Crime and Punishment**, Nusser gives no examples to clarify his distinctions. What he does instead is quote other critics. The chapter on the history of the genre is primarily the history of Anglo-Saxon detective fiction, although Nusser numbers Francois Gayot de Pitaval's true-crime history, **Causes célèbres et intéressantes, avec les jugements qui les ont décidées** (1734-1743), as one of the genre's literary forerunners.

For readers already familiar with English-language book-length treatments of the genre, the most informative parts of Nusser's book are his chapters on the structure and the psycho-sociological effects of detective novels, as well as the twenty-five bibliographies of secondary sources, roughly one at the end of each chapter subsection. But, overall, Nusser has tried to do too much. Perhaps because of the attempt at comprehensiveness, errors have crept in, such as the statement that Carter Brown is an American spin-off from Hammett and Chandler (p. 135), or that Robert L. Fish and Robert L. Pike are pennames of Ed McBain (p. 137). Also, Nusser tries to argue taxonomy with other critics without ever naming examples (other than **Crime and Punishment**) (pp. 1-25). Elsewhere he discusses the well-known "detective story and democracy" theme without mentioning Russian mystery authors such as Marietta Sergejewna Schaginjan or Wenjamin Alexandrowitsch Kawerin, both of whom wrote in the 1920s and both of whose books have German translations. And nowhere is Asian detective literature mentioned. Most of Nusser's documentation is of secondary sources; this is so much the case, and he uses them so frequently when he should mention detective **novels,** that one gets the unmistakable impression that he is more familiar with the critical literature than with the genre itself. However, as an overview of the critical literature on the topics Nusser discusses, the book is excellent. The twenty-five bibliographies of secondary sources, covering four or five languages, make the book almost worth the DM 16.80 (= $6.95), even if one does not read German. (Greg Goode)

Über Eric Ambler. Compiled and edited by the editors of Diogenes Verlag. (Diogenes Taschenbuch 187.) Zurich: Diogenes Verlag AG, 1979, 192 pp.

Über Eric Ambler is a part of a German series of essay anthologies on writers, many of whom are mystery writers. The series includes books on William Faulkner, Friedrich Durrenmatt, Simenon, and Patricia Highsmith. The book on Ambler includes German translations of commentary and essays by German, French, British, and American writers: Aurel Schmidt, Jürgen Busche, Helmet Heissenbüttel, Hans C. Blumemberg, the French mystery critic Francis Lacassin, Gabriel Veraldi, Paxton Davis, and, last but not least, Alfred Hitchcock. In addition to these critical pieces, there is quite a bit of non-critical material by and about Ambler: an Ambler short story, an interview, a short bibliography, bibliographies of primary and secondary sources, a filmography, and an autobiographical photo-essay prepared by Ambler specifically for this book. Most of the essays come from newspapers, magazines, or forewords to Ambler's books, and all of the material not originally written in German has been translated into German.

The critical essays are very interesting and the European critical outlook quite enlightening. Ambler is called a forerunner of the French **nouveau roman,** he is compared to Hitchcock, he is argued to have had a profound influence on the films of Orson Welles, and it is asserted that he did for the modern spy novel what Hammett did for the murder mystery. Almost all the critics praise Ambler's realism and the acuity with which he sketches political situations. Many of the critics argue that Ambler's books are Literature.

The bibliographies, filmography, and photo-essay alone, however, are worth the price of the book (DM 6.80, roughly $2.75), even if one does not read German. British, American, and German edition information is given for the novels, essay collections, and short story anthologies. The filmography includes Ambler's screenplays, teleplays, and the films taken from his novels. The bibliography of secondary sources includes reference books, interviews, essays, and longish book reviews. The photo-essay contains many "rare" photos of Ambler, even a baby picture. With all the information in it, this book is one of the best in the Diogenes series and makes one strongly wish that English and American paperback houses would attempt a similar project. (Greg Goode)

Janwillem van de Wetering. **The Butterfly Hunter.** Houghton Mifflin, 1982, $12.95.

Although it is billed as "a novel of suspense," **The Butterfly Hunter** is really an episodic telling of the life of Eddie Sachs. Van de Wetering achieves some suspense by evoking a memorable character in whose fate we are interested but with whom we have no sympathy. Eddie is never a likable or admirable figure.

Early in his life, Eddie was an agent of destruction, manipulating the death of his older half-brother while both were in their teens. He moved through periods of spying and thievery in World War II but always managed to come out all right or maybe a little ahead. Finally, in his late fifties, the threads of Eddie's life come together, putting him on the trail of $100 million in gold hidden by the Nazi's at the end of the war. The climax is fittingly ironic, exposing layers of blood and betrayal. While **The Butterfly Hunter** is not up to the standards of the de Gier and Grijpstra novels, it is a gripping adventure novel, studying the greed and amorality of men. (Fred Dueren)

Janwillem van de Wetering. **The Butterfly Hunter.** Houghton Mifflin, 1982, 218 pp., $12.95.

This is not a mystery story, and even the sub-title "a novel of suspense" needs some explanation, which is partly supplied in the statement by William Kotzwinkle on the back of the dust jacket that **The Butterfly Hunter** is "a work of Zen art ... filled with insight into the cynical and amusing nature of man." This characterization may serve as a caution to the reader not to expect conventional treatment; it also serves to raise some interesting questions about the purpose and the province of suspense fiction in general.

The main character, Eddy Sachs, is a completely empty person who spends a lifetime in an effort to find an identity for himself, adopting the roles of the people he destroys, and permitting himself no commitments beyond those that contribute to his own satisfaction. He makes an especially strong identification with Absalom, the biblical son of David, who tried to steal his father's throne and who is the subject of the Rembrandt painting that becomes the center of the sordid conspiracy which supplies the basis for the plot of the story.

The Butterfly Hunter is rich in van de Wetering's characteristically skillful handling of symbolic imagery, especially in the way in which the Rembrandt painting of the "golden king," as he is called in the story, becomes a symbol for the ruthless quest of Eddy Sachs after a multi-million-dollar cache of buried Nazi gold. Eddy progressively identifies with Absalom, first in his attempt to destroy the painting, later when he recognizes the almost literal parallel between his life and that of the rebellious son of David, and finally when he and the Rembrandt are destroyed together. Like most of van de Wetering's other stories, this one is heavy with dream-symbolism, including the device he has used previously, the parallel dreams of the three main characters, each of which constitutes an insight into his or her basic motivations.

The story is extremely well told. The only question is whether
[Continued on page 31]

The Documents In the Case (Letters)

From Jim Traylor, 2100 Mark Hall Court, Marietta, GA 30062:

I'm always impressed with the quality of the articles and the reviews, but it seems that I like the letters most. In this issue [7:1] I was struck with the one from John Reilly. I, as most of us, have used many bibliographies, etc., and the quibbles which most of the people (and critics) raised about that monumental and helpful book are asinine. I literally blessed him the day I found the book and his decision to include short stories (etc.) from the pulps and elsewhere. I'd have been hard pressed to find out any details about Carroll John Daly without him (this was all pre-Hagemann, of course). The two lead articles on **Black Mask** and the pulps by Bob Sampson were quite well done. I always enjoy Sampson because he throws off more knowledge of the pulps than I possess.

From Frank Denton, 14654 8th Ave. S.W., Seattle, WA 98166:

The Mystery Fancier, vol. 7, no. 2, arrived just in time to get put into a box of reading and writing material to be taken to our cabinet for the Memorial Day weekend. Unfortunately, the reading didn't last that long. It was over too quickly.

This was an excellent issue. For me, personally, the highest marks would go to Jane Bakerman's "An Interview With Desmond Bagley." It's truly a shame that Mr. Bagley died recently. Unless there is a book published posthumously, Bakerman's listing of the novels will be a handy bibliography to keep near. Bagley's mention of a biographical work, **Writer,** leads one to hope that it may have been complete enough to bear publishing. I have a friend in England, science fiction writer Keith Roberts, who met Bagley one time a couple of years ago at his publisher's office. As I recall, they had lunch together and seemed to hit it off fairly well. Keith described Bagley as friendly, affable, an excellent conversationalist, and from his own reading of the novels, as one heck of a good writer. Fifteen books, a substantial list, but all too short. Desmond Bagley will be missed. I have a videotape of **Running Blind,** filmed in Iceland and featuring many Icelandic actors and actresses. It's a visual tribute to Bagley's use of setting and has borne up well under repeated viewings. Does anyone know of any other Bagley novels which have been made into film or television features?

May I correct an error in Alan Mosier's excellent overview of recent Sherlockiana? John Gardner, who wrote the very fine **Return of Moriarty** and **The Revenge of Moriarty**, is the English John Gardner and is not dead. So we may yet have a third Moriarty book. He's well known for his "Boysie Oakes" novels and others. At the moment, however, he is busily making bucks as the author of three new James Bond novels, having been chosen by the Fleming Estate for that task. Having not read the books, I can report only that the reviews were so-so on the first book, somewhat negative on the second, and more favorable on the third, the recent **Icebreaker**.

The John Gardner whom Mosier speaks of as having recently died is the American John Gardner, author of **Grendel, The Sunlight Dialogues, The King's Indian, Mikkelson's Ghost, Moral Fiction,** and other works. He died in a motorcycle accident, and was only in his mid-forties, I believe. A loss to American mainstream fiction.

I enjoyed, as usual, Marv Lachman's overview of non-fiction books about our genre and Walter Albert's damsel-in-distress film overview. I think, perhaps, that I don't like such films any more than Walter does.

I don't know if I can agree with Melinda Reynolds or not. The women authors whom she lists are not my favorites either. But I have enjoyed many novels by two British women, Elizabeth Lemarchand and June Thomson. And Martha Grimes, an American who has written three novels in English settings with an English detective, has charmed the socks right off of me. She and John R.L. Anderson are my two most recent finds.

Thanks especially for a very nice memorial about Jud Sapp. It was nicely done and is an excellent tribute to his spot in mystery fandom.

The computer produces beautiful copy. You could have told those of us who own computers or use such what you bought, what word processing program you are using and what printer. Walter called me a couple of weeks back to chat about our Eagle IIs. I love mine, and boy, does it take the drudgery out of typing drafts. Your magazine is a real beaut now and Brad Foster is a gem of a find. I've admired his work in sf fanzines and you are, indeed, lucky to get him to do covers for you.

[**Asking a new computer owner about his machines is as risk-ridden as asking a parent about his children—out comes the wallet, quick as a flash, and the monotonous showing of snapshots competes with interminable anecdotes about their cute doings to bore you into a stupor. I'll try to restrain myself.**

I bought my computer after a search that lasted nearly three years. I had a few basic requirements in mind from the beginning. First, it had to have at least one disk drive, and preferably two, so that the documents I typed up could be stored and edited at leisure. Second, it had to be able to produce proportional-spaced, right-margin-justified copy. And third, I had to be able to afford it. Three years back I could find systems that met the first two requirements, but not the third. Ten thousand dollars seemed to be about the size of it, although, by skimping here and sacrificing there and generally being willing to accept something other than what I really wanted, I could have knocked it down to six or seven thou. So I waited, all the time keeping an eye on the market. And, sure enough, the prices declined steadily, and—what was even more surprising—the capabilities of the lower-priced machines increased at the same time.

One of the machines that I had been looking at from the beginning was the Radio Shack Model III, the 48K model with two disk drives. The problem with it, besides its limited memory, was that no software existed for it which could produce both proportional spacing and right-margin-justification at the same time. The Radio Shack boys kept saying that it would be available within a month or so—but they kept saying that for a couple of years. When I first looked at it, the Model III carried a price tag of $2495; its word-processing program was $199; a diasy-wheel printer was $1995, and the cord to hook it all together was $39.95. Total cost—$4728.95, unless I've miskeyed my pocket calculator. And it wouldn't do what I needed.

Well, as other companies improved their offerings, Radio Shack began to drop its price on the Model III (RS was in the process of developing another machine to take the place of the Model III, though this did not become common knowledge until quite recently). First, it dropped to $2295, then to $1995, and then, early this year, to $1795, and there may have been a price drop since then. More importantly, Radio Shack finally put together a word-processing program which could simultaneously support proportional spacing and right-margin justification. At this point I was very seriously considering purchasing a setup from Radio Shack.

And then I read about the Osbourne I. I had, in fact, seen an article about this chap Osbourne in a computer magazine several years ago. The gist of the article was that was he hard at work putting together a portable (as in portable-sewing-machine sized, c. thirty pounds portable) computer with dual disk drives and 64K internal memory which he intended to market for under $2000. Fat chance, I thought at the time, and that seems to have been the general thrust of the article as well.

Only Osbourne did it. For $1795. Complete with hundreds and hundreds of dollars worth of free software, including one of the most popular word-processing programs on the market—Word Star. Hot damn! I said, or words more or less to that effect, and I hied myself off to the nearest Osbourne dealer for a demonstration. The machine did all it was advertised to do, but it was afflicted with a tiny 5" screen which was guaranteed to cause headaches after half an hour or less of steady peering. Still, a separate twelve-inch monitor could be added on for another $150 or so, and I was on the verge of buying an Osbourne I when I saw an article about portable computers in another magazine. This article evaluated eight or ten portables and seemed to give the best marks to a maverick called a Kaypro II. It was the same price as the Osbourne, but it came with a nine-inch screen and an even more attractive package of software.

To come finally to the point, I went up to Indianapolis to look at the machine, found the nine-inch screen to be quite comfortable to read, was overwhelmed by the $3,000 worth of software that was thrown in to sweeten the deal (including Perfect Writer [word processing], Perfect Filer [which I use for my mailing list], and The Word Plus [a dictionary (among other things) which makes catching and correcting misspellings a snap] and a handful of other programs which I may never have any use for), and decided then and there to buy it. But I still needed a printer. No trouble, the friendly computer salesman said, I've got a beauty of a daisy-wheel printer called the Transtar 130 which sells for $895. I couldn't believe it. The cheapest daisy-wheel printer I had seen anywhere else was the one that Radio Shack was selling for $1995. But I looked at it, and it worked beautifully, so I bought it, too. [Its only flaw is its awful slowness—a snail-like sixteen characters per second, which is only about twice my normal typing speed.] So, after I purchased several dozen disks and several dozen ribbons, I found myself in business after spending a mere

$3,000. [And to think that I could have taken up match-book collecting as a hobby, instead of amateur publishing ....]

The other day, just as I was congratulating myself on having held out until I could get exactly what I wanted for the lowest possible price, I noticed that a new computer store in nearby Columbus, Indiana, was offering the Kaypro II to the public for $1595. Oh, well ....

But I am quite pleased with the machine and the software, and I would strongly recommend that anyone contemplating committing computercide take a good long look at the Kaypro before spending more money on anything else. Now I'll put my snapshots away and get back to the business at hand—more letters.]

From Jane S. Bakerman, R.R. 23, Box 131, Terre Haute, IN 47802:

Yes, certainly, of course! Jim Goodrich and all other members of **The Mystery Fancier** gang (and probably their friends and relatives) are certainly welcome to become members of the Popular Culture Association. Simply send $20.00 (which includes both membership fees and subscription to the **Journal of Popular Culture**) to: Popular Culture Association, Center for the Study of Popular Culture, Popular Culture Building, Bowling Green State University, Bowling Green, OH 43403. Next year's meeting will be in Toronto, and the general chair will be Barrie Hayne, one of the best of the terrific Mystery/Detection crowd who frequent these annual meetings. In recent years the entire conference has included about 1,000 presentations, a good many of them--at least thirty, often more--dealing with mystery fans' most beloved subjects: mystery writers and mystery fiction. Additionally, hosts of other interesting presentations on multitudes of subjects are available to any member present. The talk is good; the people are cordial--read name tags and introduce yourself without hesitation--and we enjoy ourselves mightily and learn a lot! A PCA membership will bring further details of these national (and also regional) meetings.

I much appreciated, Guy, your comment upon the death of Desmond Bagley who, like Jud Sapp, will be sorely missed. In the business of interviewing, one's encounters are generally pleasant, often warm. Both Desmond and Joan Bagley were very welcoming to me, offering entertainment and hospitality as well as information. I value the two days' worth of memories they gave me. The Bagleys are high on my list of "good people."

And, TMF looks very, very spiffy these days. Good work!

From Melinda Reynolds, Rt. 2, Box 93B, Corydon, KY 42406:

TMF arrived yesterday and I took some time to read through it. Aside from the Kildare article, I found this issue very entertaining and informative.

I especially like the review sections (books, movies, TV, whatever); with extra spending money in short supply, I find it very helpful to read what a prospective book or movie is about before spending the money and discovering the book or movie wasn't what I thought it was--and vice versa, I might find out that a book or movie I didn't think would interest me would, through the reviews, turn out to be something I would enjoy.

Also, the new format looks great; your time, money, and effort have been well spent, and you have a fanzine to be proud of. And not only does it look marvelous, you can probably get even more stuff into each issue.... Nice cover again; can we look forward to more art from Brad W. Foster? [I dearly hope so.]

I approve of your placing the article on women writers in the Letters section; I think you may get much more response to it there, as it's much more fun to carry out a "debate" in the letters section, than to comment on an article.

Re Philip T. Asdell's letter, page 42: I agree completely! Giving credit for detective fiction is almost as bad as offering credit on courses studying the works of science fiction.

Linda Toole, page 46, wanted to know if she was the only subscriber to read less than 1000 words a minute, and doubted the claim of others to read a book in a few hours. I don't know about everyone else, but reading a novel in two hours is fairly easy for me; but, I have also taken as long as six hours to read an average size book--I flinch at the thought of reading a book that is over 300 pages (hardcover). It takes me longer to read a paperback than a hardback, and if it's a book I like I usually take longer reading it on the second and third go arounds. Whenever I try to time myself to see what my reading speed is, I become more conscious of the seconds passing than of what I'm reading--but in all my classes I usually finished reading assignments before the rest of the class; however, my writing and typing speed is very slow, so I guess it all evens out.

From Greg Goode, Hahnenstr. 27, Bl, Zi. 221, 5030 Hürth-Efferen, West Germany:

TMF 7:2 is an excellent issue in many ways. First, it looks just great, and it's got running page headings too, which are a great help. This particular issue was a forum of controversial opinion: Walter Albert spoke out against damsel-in-distress films, Philip Asdell came out against college courses on detective fiction, Fred Isaac against a schism in fandom, and Joe Christopher and Bob Randisi against **TMF** itself! But most of all, my hat goes off to Marvin Lachman and Melinda Reynolds for perhaps courageously voicing what may be the most controversial opinions of all. I agree with Marvin about the boring nature of the wrong kind of academic writing. Period. But as for Melinda Reynolds"s frank, interesting letter, I agree that many women writers are too cutsey-cosy and wordy. But perhaps Ms. Reynolds should try Dorothy Uhnak, Marcia Muller, or maybe Helen MacInnes.

Thanks to Alan Mosier's article on Sherlockian pastiches, for he mentioned **Sherlock Holmes and the Golden Bird** which, because of its character Chu San Fu, I'll have to find and add to my collection of Sinister Oriental lore.

Funny Bob Adey should review Friedrich Dürrenmatt's novel **The Judge and His Hangman**. A while ago I read some German articles on Dürrenmatt's "krimis." He is thought in Germany to be the best writer of crime novels there is. He is written about quite a lot. In various articles whose style would make Marvin Lachman find comfort in that of the "wrong" **English-language** academics, Dürrenmatt is credited with having brought about the destruction of the crime novel as well as fostering an "anti-enlightenment" with respect to the genre. In the opinion of many German critics, almost all of whom are academics, the only English-language writer who can compare to Dürrenmatt is Chandler.

As I saw the editorial comment about the death of Desmond

Bagley, my initial reaction wavered between sadness and disbelief. I'm very glad to see Jane Bakerman's interview with Bagley. I was sincerely waiting, eagerly waiting, for his next book. More than any other writer of suspense/High Adventure, Bagley has the ability to pull the reader on by exciting his curiosity and stimulating his sense of wonder. He takes one on thought-adventures merely by providing his endlessly intriguing backgrounds. And this is all in addition to the suspense in all his work, which builds up like steam in a pressure cooker.

Along with Jim Goodrich I can suggest some cover motifs since the covers will change every time and since Brad Foster is so capable. How about detective caricatures, Golden Age art deco, Oriental gothic (like the title backdrops in the Chan films), movie scene mock-ups, and covers in the style of vintage paperbacks, especially the lushly garish, attention-grabbing style of Handi-Books, which were among the most striking of vintage covers. It's interesting that science fiction and fantasy both have characteristic "looks"; there is even sf art. It would be nice if our genre developed something of the sort.

From Katherine M. Restaino, Dean, Saint Peter's College/Englewood Cliffs, Englewood Cliffs, NJ 07632:

I enjoyed reading **The Mystery Fancier** very much. My favorite sections are book reviews and the letters.

I feel I should respond to Philip T. Asdell's letter regarding courses in detective fiction. I don't think that courses in detective fiction, offered at many colleges and universities as electives, will ruin our educational system. Courses in detective fiction, science fiction, and film (to mention just a few of the "modern horrors") do not replace Shakespeare, plant physiology, or calculus. The bastardization of education comes not from offering courses in detective fiction, but rather from reducing science courses from lab to non-lab courses, offering "baby math" instead of calculus, and replacing modern language requirements for the degrees with courses in foreign literature in translation.

After all these years, it is rather late to deplore the fact that colleges offer degrees in business, hotel administration, and home economics. Liberal Arts faculty members have to live with these disciplines and can do so if they bring enlightenment and enrichment into literature, both in popular and classic forms.

Detective fiction is taught for many reasons, not just for the purpose of providing a mirror of cultural, social, or popular history. Courses in detective fiction help a student deal with the problems of deciding a genre and its subdivisions. A student will be able to learn the intricacies of plot development and they are taught to apply critical standards.

There is hope for courses in detective fiction, especially if one wants to go back to the beginning with **Oedipus**, one of the earliest detective stories.

From Teri White, 3280 Lansmere, Shaker Heights, OH 44122:

I can find not a thing with which to disagree in Melinda Reynolds' letter about women writers. For years just the name of a female author on a book was enough for me to return it immediately to the shelf. Ms. Reynolds makes some entirely valid points about aspects of the books. What always infuriated me the most was reading reviews of such books--said reviews usually written by men (a gender in which some of my best friends are) and proclaiming a book "a woman's story." Not this woman, thank you very much.

Admittedly, as a confirmed feminist in all other aspects of my life, this stand against women writers occasionally causes me a twinge of pain.

Having said all that, I must now say that grim as the situation has been in the past, it is changing. I suggest that Ms. Reynolds move into more contemporary work. I have found in the recent past a number of women turning out work that ranks with the best. Nicely hard-boiled in a number of cases. A few names to illustrate my point: Julie Smith, Sara Paretsky, Marcia Muller, Sue Grafton, and Liza Cody are some names that come immediately to mind. To a greater or lesser degree, these authors have all written books that even a tough broad like myself can enjoy.

Let's hope that more and more women see fit to break out of the genteel ghetto of crime writing where they've been for so long, and make their way in the real mean streets.

From Jeff Banks, Box 13007 SFA Sta., Nacogdoches, TX 75962:

Herewith, a couple more reviews. My reviews are scarce as hen's teeth, I know, and I feel a bit like a veterinarian-dentist specializing in hens whenever I sit down to write one nowadays. I am reading much more the last three years than ever before, but I am also getting to be a much more critical reader.

I love Marty Wooster's reviews; even when I don't agree with him (as is often the case) I find his arguments well reasoned. But I do not want to be **TMF**'s second critic. For all that every fanzine needs one, few could survive two.

In short, my recent reading has been more for what I can learn than what I can enjoy; that (perhaps) is making me much harder to please. When I can be enthusiastic, I will send you a review occasionally.

Needless to say, I enjoyed your most recent issue. I've come to expect to.

Even though I make a fetish of avoiding writing fannish l.o.c.s, **TMF** nearly always tempts me. Did again this time, but no time. Where does it all go?

From Frank Floyd, Rt. 3, Box 139-F, Berryville, AR 72616:

I am in your debt for sending Vol. 7, No. 1. Having gone through a moving, I had simply gotten out of touch (yet, to complain to such a one as yourself about moving, who am I, a mere nothing?); however, I still receive most of my mail at my old address, by choice. I had decided that **The Mystery Fancier** had been a victim of unkind fate.

None of my time in reading and studying the issue was other than well spent. Hagemann's "Captain Joseph T. Shaw's Black Mask Scrapbook" was good; I liked Bob Sampson's "Detection by Other Means" too. On a par with these in interest, I thought, was the letter from John M. Reilly. I enjoyed the letter from Ola Strom.

From Fred Dueren, Box 7662, Shawnee Mission, KS 66207:

Can you add the following note for me in the letters section? I'm selling off quite a few of my collection, a lot of the non-series, hard-boiled and spy stuff. I'm sending the sale list to anyone from TMF whose address I have, but if any readers didn't get a copy and want one, they can write to me at [the above address] and I'll be glad to send it.

[Fred sent me a copy of the list, which runs to nine pages. His prices are very, very reasonable—except for two $3 items, the highest price is $2.50, and most or less than that, including the paperbacks, which run about a buck or less apiece.]

From Donald Ireland, A1 Crime Fiction, 25 Acreman Court, Sherborne, Dorset, DT9 3PW, ENGLAND:

Am never certain whether you accept "advertisements" [I don't] or whether you just put notes in your magazine [I do].
I would be grateful--if you accept advertisements to put this in--or if you don't to give A1 Crime a mention.[...]
We are specialists in the Crime-Detective field. Over 8,000 books in stock. Lists issued monthly. "Wants" very much a proven specialty.

From Jon Breen, 10642 La Bahia Ave, Fountain Valley, CA 92708:

I see by the latest **Mystery Fancier** that you have acquired a word processor. The results look great. The content of the latest issue is also very good.
I probably will not be the only one to point out a rather serious error in Alan S. Mosier's good article on Sherlockian pastiche. The John Gardner who died in an accident was the American novelist, a non-mystery writer though he certainly used elements of the form in his last novel, **Mikkelsson's Ghosts**. Still alive and well as far as I know is the British John Gardner who wrote the Moriarty series and is currently turning out new James Bonds.... Re Marv Lachman's always worthwhile column: The husband of the Kelley Roos team was William Roos. Audrey Kelley was the maiden name of the late Mrs. Roos.
Bob Randisi's list of the top ten private eyes is bound to arouse controversy. Actually, it's not at all a bad list of the best of the contemporary crop, but I can't see how he can claim many (or indeed any) of them are superior to Philip Marlowe. And how could he leave Ross Macdonald's Lew Archer out? (Many of the characters on his list owe an **awesome** debt to both Marlowe and Archer.) Okay to leave off Sam Spade, but surely Hammett should at least be represented by the Continental Op. If it were my list, I'd be inclined to make a place for Brett Halliday's Mike Shayne, whose cases are excellent at their best and whose reputation has suffered at the hands of the large group of writers (though there are some good ones among them) who have described his activities since Halliday became a house name. I'll definitely second Bob, though, on his high opinion of "Nameless" and his pointed omission of Spenser.

www.ingramcontent.com/pod-product-compliance
Lightning Source LLC
Chambersburg PA
CBHW031435040426
42444CB00006B/817